Beyond the
Glass Slipper

TEN NEGLECTED FAIRY TALES TO FALL
IN LOVE WITH

INTRODUCTION AND ANNOTATIONS BY
KATE WOLFORD

World Weaver Press

Published by World Weaver Press
Kalamazoo, Michigan
www.WorldWeaverPress.com

Edited by Eileen Wiedbrauk
Interior and cover layout designed by World Weaver Press

First Edition: April 2013

ISBN-13: 978-0615797359
ISBN-10: 0615797350

For Todd, my husband, who is more than a prince.

CONTENTS

BEYOND THE GLASS SLIPPER

INTRODUCTION

A pretty girl sleeps on and on. We wonder if she dreams. An angry little man makes gold from straw. We wonder why he barters for a child. Seven dwarfs live in a cottage. We want to name them. A fish girl longs for a land man. We want her to land him. A vegetable touches the clouds. We want to climb it. A wheezing beast stares longingly at a beautiful girl who nervously tries to eat. We hope she will find a way to love him, tusks and all.

Images from classic fairy tales inspire and compel audiences the world over and have done so for centuries. "Sleeping Beauty," "Rumpelstiltskin," "Snow White," "Jack and the Beanstalk," "Beauty and the Beast"—all are integrated into our cultural DNA. We ramble on about rescue fantasies and evil stepmothers and five magic beans, because the twenty or so fairy tales that define the genre are so popular that they obscure the joys of the thousands of other fairy tales from across the world and time.

The allure of the major tales is pretty potent, and the supremacy of the big ones in popular culture is understandable. But serious fairy tale lovers know there is undiscovered treasure in the pokey corners of public libraries and on the internet, where hardcore fairy tale fans and dedicated scholars labor to unearth, read, and discuss neglected tales. Those of us who dig, discover that many fairy tales do not feature Princes Charming, that as many as half of fairy tales have male protagonists, that fairies don't show up all that much in "fairy" tales, and that bad behavior is rewarded nearly as often as good behavior.

Although this book will deal with European fairy tales, fascinating fairy tales can be found the world over. The most popular fairy tales emerged from Western Europe, but their prevalence says more about market forces than about the diversity or even quality of fairy tales in general. Popular fairy tales are the result of demand by audiences. "The Little Mermaid" by Hans Christian Andersen, is not a more entertaining story than "The Girl Who Trod on the Loaf," also by Andersen. Yet people who bought and read fairy tales, over time, clearly liked the story of a mermaid who yearns for a man and a soul more than the story of a vain little girl who spends countless years as a statue in the Devil's waiting room. Both stories revel in horrible detail about the tortures the two young girls endure, and both reflect Andersen's moral and spiritual beliefs. But the mermaid, who is a suicide for love in Andersen's version, is one of the most famous fairy-tale heroines in the world, and has been for generations. The girl with the loaf is a curiosity that, in the United States, at least, is not well known outside of fairy tale circles. The public made the choice to love one more than the other.

Here's the thing about the fairy tales we have made popular: we shape them at least as much as they shape us. No one made people flock to Disney's *Snow White* in the 1930s or the 40s or the 90s and beyond. Disney did not lasso people into theaters to watch a film that in many ways is very different than the tale the Brothers Grimm set down. Disney did make a film that changed the dwarfs from very tidy men with no names to the famously-monikered gang that fears soap the way the Evil Queen fears laugh lines, but audiences endorsed it and cemented it into popular culture. Snow White as a housekeeping dynamo with a super-maternal spirit is a twentieth-century American creation, not a nineteenth-century German one.

More Is Better

We lament the messages fairy tales send, yet we lap them up. Feminist critics have found fairy tales to be a rich hunting ground for examining the truths and burdens placed on women by a patriarchal society. Who can blame them? Fairy tales *do* endorse patriarchy and retrograde notions about women and their behavior. In "Fairy Gifts," we see fairy tales that caution against women being too pretty, too witty, too talkative, and too flirty—in just one tale. We also see princesses married to men they do not know and who could not possibly truly care for them. In "The Dirty Shepherdess," the heroine boldly and honestly proclaims her love for her father in a way that displeases him, yet she meekly leaves when he orders her to. In "The Loving Pair," Ball (a toy), who is female, remains forever in a rain gutter because she is apparently too damaged to be of worth. The message in "The Loving Pair" is clear: when a woman is "ruined," that's the end.

Clearly, people who worry about the messages fairy tales send to women have good reason to think the way they do. But fairy tales that uphold old-fashioned gender roles can also send important messages about strong women. Women are the sole focus in "Fairy Gifts," which is also in this volume. The Flower Fairy has the power. The princesses the heroine visits have their own royal courts, even if they also have some deplorable personal traits, like being too talkative. Women are what matters in this tale, and in many fairy tales, women may get burdensome messages, but they also get the lion's share of attention. Men may have most of the power in life and in fairy tales, but women get a lot of attention and the word count in life and in fairy tales.

Take "Kisa the Cat," an Icelandic fairy tale adapted by Andrew Lang in the late 1800s and featured here. Kisa is strong, wily, decisive, caring, and focused. She's a human princess enchanted into cat form who takes on a giant and reattaches a princess's chopped-off feet via magical surgery. She and the human princess she cares for, Ingibjorg, have a friendship that transcends species and Ingibjorg's marriage. Sure, both women get married, but that was the career path open to royal women. What the two princesses have as friends is clearly what's important in the story. Princes? They are an afterthought. A necessary, but trivial, detail.

Feminist criticism is only one exciting and vital area of fairy tale scholarship. Historical, science-based, sociological, and psychoanalytical criticism have all flourished or continue to. There's room in fairy tale scholarship for myriad approaches and that's what makes it fun and challenging. *Beyond the Glass Slipper* is not a scholarly work, so forms of criticism will not be in the spotlight. Yet, in nearly ten years of using fairy tales to teach college writing, I have found that male students love fairy tales, but don't necessarily believe they have any stake in fairy tale study and culture.

That's not the fault of any school of criticism. No area of fairy tale criticism I've encountered tries to marginalize any group of readers. That men don't feel much connection with fairy tales may be the result of Disney princess culture, but it may also be the result of fairy tales being assigned to children's literature. Almost all of my students are shocked to find that many fairy tales were not written specifically for children. They are appalled, both men and women, when I "ruin" decent, innocent children's stories by discussing earlier texts of classic fairy tales. Shame on me! Yet, wrongly, I think, children's literature and by extension, fairy tales, are considered less important than adult literature. And since women have traditionally raised children, fairy tales and children's literature are thought to be solely women's work by many students, male and female.

Why worry about men and fairy tales at all? After all, men have always been in fairy tale studies. Right at the forefront, and I don't just mean the Brothers Grimm and Bruno Bettelheim. Men not only criticize and study fairy tales, they rewrite them and create new fairy tales, as do women. Yet my audience both in the classroom and at *Enchanted Conversation*, the online blogazine I publish, is largely female, and I don't think it's just because more college students are women and women read fiction more than men. The most famous fairy tales are women centered. There's "Snow White," "Sleeping Beauty," "Rapunzel," "The Little Mermaid," and "Beauty and the Beast." "Aladdin" is certainly famous, as is "Jack and the Beanstalk," but the most popular and culturally influential tales are about girls. Even so, many young women avoid reading fairy tales because the most popular fairy tales carry a lot of baggage about the messages they send women

People want to read stories about people who are like them, with ideas about life that speak to them, specifically. People also get sick of reading the same stories over and over again. The great news is, many fairy tales aren't just about princesses under the sea and in towers. Fairy tales take place in gloomy underground passages, people turn into animals and have adventures, ghosts show up in fairy tales, nasty people sometimes win in fairy tales. Soldiers are popular characters in fairy tales, as are millers' sons. Kings get deposed and pigs get married and turn into gorgeous princes. And, while fairy tales appear to endorse business as usual in terms of power and social order, much sly subversiveness takes place before authority reassumes command—if it does.

Beyond the Glass Slipper features ten fairy tales that are largely invisible to fairy-tale lovers who are not deeply immersed in the field. Much of my professional life is focused on fairy tales, and yet, I was unfamiliar with some of the stories before starting this project.

They are wildly different from many well-known tales, and because of their scope and unfamiliarity, give readers a solid view of the diversity of fairy tales (and these are only a few European ones).

Readers will, perhaps, also see how flexible fairy tales are in terms of message and content, which in turn, will show them that fairy tales are for everyone. They are for little kids, old folks, teenagers, kids in the city, farmers, hipster dudes, college students, kids who love anime and people who just love fantasy. Fairy tales are magical and funny and beautiful. They are for everyone, but not everyone knows that.

Few fairy tales are love stories, but the point of *Beyond the Glass Slipper* is to make readers fall in love with obscure, strange, even twisted fairy tales. For those of us who passionately love these stories, fairy tales are not optional in life, because they are human life in its many crazy manifestations. I am evangelical on fairy tales because they continue to expand my view of how life may be lived. I read their messages, even the preachy, annoying ones, and develop my own ideas about love and power and money, and the way fairy tales mix things up gives me new perspective every time I read a new tale.

A Little Background

For the purposes of this book, a fairy tale is a story of wonder and transformation that flourishes through speaking, writing, and listening. While there are useful systems for categorizing fairy tales and folklore, they aren't the focus of this book, although sources that feature these systems are listed in the annotated bibliography. Think of what makes a fairy tale this way: it's hard to define, but you'll know one when you read it.

The origins of fairy tales are murky. Like ancient Greek and Roman myths, the earliest fairy tales cannot be pinpointed. Hints and glimmers of what would become fairy tales can be found in a story called "Tale of Two Brothers." It's an Ancient Egyptian story from over a thousand years prior to the Common Era. In addition, *Aesop's Fables*, probably written in Ancient Greece about 500 years before the Common Era, has a folktale sort of appeal as well as the sense of wonder we often feel when reading fairy tales, even if they aren't the latter. The following information is a very small peek into what we may know about early fairy tales, in the West.

We do know that some ancient stories, like "Cupid and Psyche" seem to echo in fairy tales like the later Norwegian fairy tale, "East of the Sun, West of the Moon." The formalized story of "Cupid and Psyche" is attributed to Lucius Apuleius, who wrote *The Golden Ass* in the second century. "Cupid and Psyche" is a tale within Apuleius's greater work, *The Golden Ass*, and is a narrative filled with much complicated trouble for poor Psyche, whose travails begin when Venus becomes jealous of the heroine's fabulous beauty. There's a happily ever after for Cupid and Psyche, but the story contains the elements of trials and tribulations that many fairy tale protagonists will face in stories popularized hundreds of years later.

"East of the Sun, West of the Moon" is not the only fairy tale with echoes of "Cupid and Psyche," but it's one of the most famous. As in the earlier story, curiosity is punished, dangerous travel is necessary, supernatural events transpire frequently, and a joyful ending is achieved. Both stories also feature a very mysterious bridegroom, a detail found in numerous other stories, the most notable being "Beauty and the Beast."

The Facetious Nights of Straparola, by Giovanni Francesco Straparola, was published in the early 1550s in Italy. ("Facetious" seems to mean "fun" or "enjoyable" in this case.) Structured like Giovanni Boccaccio's *The Decameron*, the collection features a variety of stories, including some fairy tales. "King Pig," one of our stories, is from Straparola. "Puss in Boots" can be traced to it as well. The book helped pave the way for later fairy tale collections, like those of Charles Perrault.

Like *The Decameron*, which was written in the 1350s and is also Italian, love and humor and clever social commentary can be found in Straparola's collection of tales told to amuse a sophisticated group of people in need of entertainment, who themselves are also storytellers. Like many "literary" fairy tales, heavy details about characters' appearance, shortcomings and adventures are featured in stories like "King Pig."

Since Straparola's work is frequently thought of as one of the important works in early modern fairy tale history, this seems as good a place as any to discuss the difference between "literary" and "oral" fairy tales. There is, I think, not as much of a bright line between them as many fans often believe. However, here's my own very rough way of thinking of the difference: fairy tales that seem to come from the oral tradition were initially popularized through old-fashioned word of mouth from the peasant or working classes. Literary fairy tales tend to have come from the upper classes and were popularized early on through writing and print. The important thing to remember is that fairy tales are living stories. It's true that most fairy tales are now disseminated through print, so maybe fairy tales are all a bit literary nowadays. But we still *tell* fairy tales. We act them out. We add our own details when we read them aloud. Both kinds of fairy tales remain in the twenty-first century. Below is a brief list of some authors who had major influence on fairy tales over the last four hundred years or so. Perhaps reading about them will help readers of *Beyond the Glass Slipper* begin to form their own theories on fairy tale classification.

(Please note that not everyone would agree with my ideas about oral versus literary tales. I ask readers to see my ideas as theories designed to spur them onto their own research, and, in turn, their own theories on this topic.)

Giambattista Basile wrote *Il Pentamerone; The Tale of Tales* in the 1630s. Like Straparola, he was Italian, and he also had great influence on later, more famous fairy tale collectors, for example, the Grimms. Among his notable fairy tales is "Sun, Moon, and Talia," an early, shocking, and not-to-be-missed version of "Sleeping Beauty." His version of the snoozing princess includes cannibalistic plans from her kingly lover's evil stepmother, who also tries to burn Talia alive. All ends well, but only after Talia might be wishing she had never woken up.

French literary fairy tales were popular in the seventeenth century. The best-known author of that time is Charles Perrault, whose versions of tales like "Cinderella" and "Bluebeard," are well-loved today. French literary fairy tales were popular with its upper classes, and women were notable writers of these tales. Madame D'Aulnoy wrote "The White Cat," among a number of terrific tales like "The Yellow Dwarf" and "Green Serpent." These were published in the late seventeenth century.

Both Perrault and D'Aulnoy, like Basile and Straparola, had insider knowledge of how life worked at court and among the nobility. What's notable about many of their stories is how filled with detailed descriptions of beauty and clothes and jewels and people their stories are—at least relative to the spare description found in tales with more oral traditions, such as "Little Red Riding Hood." ("Little Red Riding Hood" did get the literary treatment by Perrault, however.) Writers such as D'Aulnoy and Perrault either came from noble roots or lived their lives among the ruling classes. They were cultured and literate. And, it should be noted, both lived in Paris during the time of Louis XIV, the "Sun King." The art of conversation and enchanted storytelling were highly prized by the lucky sophisticates who participated in the salons of Paris during this time.

"Beauty and the Beast" was published in the eighteenth century, first by Gabrielle-Suzanne Barbot de Villeneuve, and then by Jeanne-Marie Le Prince de Beaumont, whose version is still popular today. Madame de Beaumont spent time as a governess, and had some bad luck in marriage before a third one, that seems to have taken. Perhaps her unhappy early marriages informed her version of "Beauty and the Beast," as a willingness to endure uncertainty and submit to the will of other people are hallmarks of Beauty's story.

The Brothers Grimm landed in the early nineteenth century, and changed folklore and fairy tales forever. Though not the only German folk and fairy tale collectors of their time, they remain the most famous and influential. The first volume of *Nursery and Household Tales* came out in 1812, and it's safe to say that fairy tales were forever changed. Jacob and Wilhelm Grimm were scholars and linguists who were passionate about German culture and history. Collecting fairy tales was an exercise in inspiring their fellow Germans to be proud of their past and culture.

To this day, many fairy tale fans believe that the Brothers Grimm transcribed their tales after hearing them directly from illiterate peasants. However, it seems pretty clear that the Grimms edited and finessed their stories quite a bit, and, the majority of their tales came from middle-class to upper-class young women. Wilhelm even married one of their sources.

Many of the stories the Brothers Grimm included in their published collections of "German" stories were popular all over Europe long before they started their work, and, as is clear in the paragraphs above, some seemingly "oral" tales like "Cinderella," had literary roots, or at least, strong influences. Even so, without the Brothers Grimm, the world of fairy tales would most likely be far poorer than it is today.

Hans Christian Andersen published his first fairy tale book in the 1830s. Eventually, his stories like "The Little Mermaid," "The Emperor's New Clothes," and "The Ugly Duckling" would become classics of children's literature. Born in Odense, Denmark, Hans was from a poor family, as his father was a shoemaker. Hans's father died while his son was quite young, so the talented youngster was forced to work and obtaining an education was difficult for him. Hans faced many obstacles and endured abuse at the hands of a cruel schoolmaster.

Hans' life as a youth and a mature man was filled (maybe even more than most people's) with emotional peaks and valleys, particularly in regard to his love life. Perhaps that's why stories such as "The Little Mermaid" (Andersen's version), break our hearts to this day. A literary success in his own day, Andersen was lauded and applauded the world over during his lifetime. Perhaps he didn't find love, but he did find immortality.

That's a pretty short review of fairy tale highlights, and it doesn't even begin to cover later achievements in the field, like *The Wizard of Oz* books. The annotated bibliography for *Beyond the Glass Slipper* features a number of books and other sources addressing the history and development of fairy tales, including their popularity in film and television, and discussions of literary fairy tales and oral fairy tales, including their histories, differences and similarities.

Moving Beyond the Glass Slipper

Beyond the Glass Slipper is an outgrowth of *Enchanted Conversation: A Fairy Tale Magazine* (fairytalemagazine.com), which debuted in January of 2009. A blogazine that publishes stories and poems with a fairy tale focus, EC is also a place for information and posts about fairy tales. Some of the most popular pieces are those *about* fairy tales—their meaning, popularity, and social significance. Whether I have written a post or a guest writer has, it's clear that people don't just want to read fairy tales; they want to think about them and discuss them.

People also want to move beyond "Cinderella," "Snow White" "Beauty and the Beast," etc. It's not that fairy tale fans don't love the most popular stories. They definitely do. But fans of any genre want to dig both deeply and widely into their subject. Yet, because there are so many fairy tales, it's hard to know where to begin when exploring beyond the canon.

It's funny, but many fairy tale readers want to move beyond the best-known stories yet don't because the sheer volume of fairy tales available these days can be overwhelming. It's easy to think, well, I'll just load up electronically on every color of Andrew Lang's fairy tale books and start reading. Then they pop up on the reader and suddenly, they just seem like too much of a good thing. I've talked to many people who collect physical and electronic editions of fairy tales, because they love fairy stories and because they want to explore their variety. But a lot of people, genuine fairy tale fans, often end up not reading the tales. Maybe this comes from too much choice. The ten stories I've chosen represent a variety of types of tales, are packed with all kinds of enchantment to ponder, and lend themselves to thoughtful discussion.

Since *Enchanted Conversation* is focused on making fairy tales something to discuss, *Beyond the Glass Slipper* is designed to inspire talking and writing about the tales. That doesn't mean that readers need to go out and discuss the stories with people—obviously not. Yet fairy tales themselves are inherently gossipy. They have a chatty, intimate quality that just begs to be talked and written about. To read a fairy tale is to be inspired and to want to share the story and the ideas it generates.

Perhaps one of the reasons fairy tales became so popular for children is that they lend themselves to reading aloud. In turn, reading aloud leads to delightful questions and interruptions, and not just from children. I like to read passages out loud when I teach. The discussions with students that follow are often the liveliest and most intriguing ones of the semester.

The advent of the internet, and for me, blogging, has given fairy-tale discourse a brand-new life. Through commenting and rating systems, it's easy to find out what excites and intrigues visitors about fairy tales. As it turns out, many things about fairy tales set people's minds in a whirl. Certainly, retellings of old tales are at the top the list, and that's a good thing, as that is one of EC's main focal points. But even more than retellings, posts that center on presenting fairy tales complete with some ideas and perspective about them are the most popular. I started writing posts fairly recently about the major fairy tales like "Beauty and the Beast," and was delighted by how well-received they were. The perspective provided about the stories seemed to be what drove the traffic, and when I realized that, the idea for this book was born.

My posts that served as the inspiration for this volume consisted of nothing more than presenting the tales in a blog post, but with introductions about what I thought about the motivations of characters like Rumpelstiltskin or the messages I thought the tales contained about power and love and parents and children. For example, I began the "Rumpelstiltskin" post like this: "Poor old Rumpelstiltskin. In my book, he was more sinned against than sinning. He always just seemed like a lonely guy who wanted a child—and really, how great would the greedy king and thoughtless miller's daughter be as parents? And the miller? A dolt. Everyone knows that you do not, do not, try to gain the attention of the greedy and powerful—unless you are attempting a palace coup."

Visitors commented, sometimes at length, on that post, as well as others with a similar structure. It dawned on me that people want to read classic tales with a bit of informal, not-too-academic commentary. Since I was already posting about the most famous fairy tales, a book of lesser-known tales, with detailed perspective, plus some provocative questioning, seemed like a project worth pursuing. And here we are.

Asking Questions, One Fairy Tale at a Time

Reader, you don't need me to tell you how to read, so I won't. But the introductions to the stories and the annotations have been designed with very specific goals in mind, so here are some important points to bear in mind when reading *Beyond the Glass Slipper:*

- Everything I have written about every tale is meant to engender thought and discussion. That's because the book is an outgrowth of the blog, *Enchanted Conversation.* Blogging and commenting are about dialogue. As a discussion leader, if you will, I am designing the introductions, questions and annotations to provoke readers. As a result, "Hey, I never thought of that!" "Are you kidding?" "I don't think that's what the story meant." "Huh?"—are all great responses to the ideas provided in this book. The comments, questions and notes are not meant to provide definitive answers. In fairy tales, there are surprisingly few definite answers. Nearly everything can be negotiated.

- While some references to scholarly sources can be found in comments and notes, this is not a scholarly work. The tone and style in *Beyond the Glass Slipper* are deliberately casual.

- As noted above, the solitary reader just looking to be entertained will likely be the main audience for *Beyond the Glass Slipper.* Yet the book is also designed for classroom use, even though it is not a deliberately scholarly work, in the sense that it contains no academic theory or extensive research of the same kind. That's a big reason why there are so many questions in the "Consider" section. I teach first-year college writing and use fairy tales as a focal point for one of my courses. (*Enchanted Conversation* has also been used for class work.) The curriculum we use demands a thesis statement grounded in evidence that comes from the synthesis of sources, but the students' own ideas are essential, paramount, even. Assignments require the use of fairy tales as primary texts and scholarly essays about fairy tales as secondary sources. Evidence has to be commented on and connected to other ideas in student essays. (We work students very hard indeed.)

Because fairy tales and teaching have been closely connected in my life, many of the questions you'll see in the "Consider" section can easily be translated into essay assignments for short papers (about three to four pages) with a few sources. For every tale, you'll see questions with suggestions for connecting other tales to the one featured. Also, the many questions sprinkled throughout the book are designed specifically to foster classroom discussion. Most importantly, every question has an implied, "Why?" That means, why do you think the way you do? Answering why is one of my favorite parts of writing.

- Book clubs will also benefit from all the questions in the "Consider" section. The sections are set up in a way that groups can start at any of the bulleted points and get a discussion going. Provocative questions about sins like greed or vanity are meant to make people put down the wineglass and start saying, "Hey, wait a minute." Or, take a big, fortifying gulp of pinot grigio after holding forth on the silliness of including a vampire story in a book about fairy tales. *Beyond the Glass Slipper* will get a club through a lively meeting with enough time for slices of decadent chocolate cake for all.

- Because *Enchanted Conversation* regularly publishes stories and poems, writers were very much on my mind during this project. If you are intrigued by the notion of writing a story or poem based on a specific fairy tale or creating a new work that is influenced by fairy tales in general, you'll find plenty of useful ideas here. The annotations and questions are designed to help writers interrogate the story for ideas on how to create new characters, details, and perspective. Sideways retellings (ones that do not just recount a classic story with some fun new details) often make the best fairy-tale-inspired new stories and poems.

- *Enchanted Conversation* will have a special section dedicated to *Beyond the Glass Slipper*, where readers of every kind can go to raise questions, share ideas and learn more about these ten fabulous stories.

- Finally, small adjustments in punctuation, etc., have been made to the tales to make them more readable. Changes have been minor and infrequent.

THE NIXY

Introduction

When we think of romantic love in fairy tales, most of us conjure up images of "true love's kiss" and glass slippers fitting just so and, of course, "happily ever after." Yet "The Nixy" takes us from before the birth of its hunter-protagonist, through his unwilling separation from his bride, past exile for both husband and wife, and into, at last, a realistic happily-ever-after ending. As such, it can be considered an antidote to the infamous fairy tale endings that readers and critics alike consider foolishly optimistic. After all, who, in even the best of marriages, ever lives in bliss for very long?

This version of "The Nixy" is from Andrew Lang's *The Yellow Fairy Book*, published in 1894. As in countless other fairy tales, it begins with a bad bargain made by a desperate parent who foolishly forgets to beware fairies bearing gifts. In this instance, the miller's future prosperity will mean relentless anxiety for himself and years of loneliness for his son.

In the case of the title character, nixies are described as mostly "wizened little beings with green skin, teeth, and hair.... They were said to have families and children under the water and to dwell in fine palaces, but their children were ugly."[†] Ah, beauty. When it comes to tales of magic, fantasy and transformation, beauty, or its lack, always lurks somewhere. Although it must be said, in the nixy's defense, that they are sometimes mermaid-like, but the pretty ones lure humans to their deaths. Some kind of ugly is always swimming about.

Beyond appearance, nixies, who tend to be found in countries like Germany and Switzerland, have the greatest power to cause harm to mortals "on St. John's Eve when the penalty for bathing in their lakes and pools is to become their eternal slave. At the spring equinox however, nixies' tears mixed with lake water are believed to bring beauty and eternal youth to the bathers."‡

In our story, despite the familiar details of troubles coming in threes and transformations and signs and portents, what's worth watching for is the message that true companionship and friendship form the bedrock of any long-term marriage or partnership. That the story *makes* the protagonists become the dearest of friends before they are truly reunited makes it an unusual fairy story. Friendship of any kind is seldom examined in well-known Western fairy tales. Since fairy tales rise to prominence, like most famous stories, based on what the audience likes, the lack of friendship as major theme in classic fairy tales says a lot about their audience.

Consider:
- The father in this tale is largely a positive, tragic figure. He pays forever, through constant anxiety, for his bargain with the nixy. Consider how different that makes him from, say, the spineless father in "Hansel and Gretel," who colludes in the destruction of his own children because his wife nags him. In the latter, the father is actually rewarded with riches from his children at the end of the story, yet there seems to be no consolation for the miller.

- Notice the unusually illustrative quality of the hunter's wife, the moon, and the golden objects during the scenes in which she is trying to lure her lost husband from the pond. Fairy tales are not often highly detailed in scene-setting, so most descriptive terms are used carefully. True, the moonlight scenes are not delineated in exhaustive detail, but they do paint a shining outline. Do these moments inspire the imagination, because, as Maria Tatar asserts, "It is actually easier to imagine human figures when they are awash in shimmering light, for they gain solidity through the contrast with insubstantiality"?[§]

- Is the nixy in this story evil? Is it possible to tell? Does it matter? She provides the name for the story, yet she disappears from the story after the flood. Her power and insubstantiality are something to think about.

- "The Nixy" could be read as a story of adultery, and how, through great sorrow and toil, a marriage can survive and even prosper after infidelity. Is the hunter's disappearance into the pond a metaphor for wandering on his part? Or, is the story about two people who start as married lovers, become strangers to one another, grow, change and grieve as long-term partners, who truly come to know each other in the end? Is it a little of both? Why? Why not? A bit more food for thought: Joan Gould writes, "Marriage involves not one transformation but a stream of transformations over time, reinforcing or opposing one another, and the fact we overlook is that time itself is a magical element."[*] How does this quote enhance an understanding of "The Nixy"?

- Is there a specific kind of happiness that is possible for the hunter and his wife at the end of the tale? We don't know what their happiness is at the end, just that it exists. How might the rest of the story be written? Would there be adventure, family, wealth? What is happiness for two people who are, truly, married friends? Can it be defined?

Source Notes

†Brasey, Edouard. *Faeries and Demons: And Other Magical Creatures.* New York: Barnes & Noble, 2003. 71.

‡Ibid, 71.

§Tatar, Maria. *Enchanted Hunters: The Power of Stories in Childhood.* New York: W.W. Norton, 2009. 75.

*Gould, Joan. *Spinning Straw into Gold: What Fairy Tales Reveal about the Transformations in a Woman's Life.* New York: Random House, 2006. 203.

THE NIXY

(From *The Yellow Fairy Book*, by Andrew Lang, 1894)

There was once upon a time a miller who was very well off, and had as much money and as many goods as he knew what to do with. But sorrow comes in the night, and the miller all of a sudden became so poor that at last he could hardly call the mill in which he sat his own. He wandered about all day full of despair and misery, and when he lay down at night[1] he could get no rest, but lay awake all night sunk in sorrowful thoughts.[2]

One morning he rose up before dawn and went outside, for he thought his heart would be lighter in the open air. As he wandered up and down on the banks of the mill-pond he heard a rustling in the water, and when he looked near he saw a white woman rising up from the waves.

He realized at once that this could be none other than the nixy of the mill-pond, and in his terror he didn't know if he should fly away or remain where he was. While he hesitated the nixy spoke, called him by his name, and asked him why he was so sad.[3]

1) *When troubles come at night, they often seem even worse than if they arrived in the day. The reference to night sets the tone for the action that is to come—much of which is after sundown. Plus, in pre-modern cultures, ghosts, ghouls, witches, etc., were seen as having more power in darkness.*

2) *The miller, a fairly sympathetic version of classic fairy tales' hapless father, is shown to be in the throes of misery and insomnia. Depicted as not in his right mind, the miller seems less culpable in making a bargain with a nixy.*

3) *The nixy speaking his name would send a powerful message to listeners who were likely familiar with the folk*

(cont.) belief that knowing someone's name gives the speaker power over the listener.

4) *There is often a big "oh no!" in fairy tales, when a parent realizes he or she has made a bargain with a kind of devil. Like Sleeping Beauty's parents, the miller will do everything in his power to save his beloved son from his terrible fate.*

When the miller heard how friendly her tone was, he plucked up heart and told her how rich and prosperous he had been all his life up till now, when he didn't know what he was to do for want and misery.

Then the nixy spoke comforting words to him, and promised that she would make him richer and more prosperous than he had ever been in his life before, if he would give her in return the youngest thing in his house.

The miller thought she must mean one of his puppies or kittens, so promised the nixy at once what she asked, and returned to his mill full of hope. On the threshold he was greeted by a servant with the news that his wife had just given birth to a boy.[4]

The poor miller was much horrified by these tidings, and went in to his wife with a heavy heart to tell her and his relations of the fatal bargain he had just struck with the nixy. "I would gladly give up all the good fortune she promised me," he said, "if I could only save my child." But no one could think of any advice to give him, beyond taking care that the child never went near the mill-pond.

So the boy throve and grew big, and in the meantime all prospered with the miller, and in a few years he was richer than he had ever been before. But all the same he did not enjoy his good fortune, for he could not forget his compact with the nixy, and he knew that sooner or later she would demand his fulfillment of it. But year after year went by, and the boy grew up and became a great hunter, and the lord of the land took him into his service, for he was as smart and bold a hunter as you would wish to see. In a short time he married a pretty young wife, and lived with her in great peace and happiness.[5]

One day when he was out hunting a hare sprang up at his feet, and ran for some way in front of him in the open field. The hunter pursued it hotly for some time, and at last shot it dead. Then he proceeded to skin it, never noticing that he was close to the mill-pond, which from childhood up he had been taught to avoid. He soon finished the skinning, and went to the water to wash the blood off his hands. He had hardly dipped them in the pond when the nixy rose up in the water, and seizing him in her wet arms she dragged him down with her under the waves.[6]

When the hunter did not come home in the evening his wife grew very anxious, and when his game bag was found close to

5) *"The Nixy" is very different from a lot of fairy tales in that it shows our hero and heroine already married and happy before their travails occur.*

6) *Drowning is a terrible fate and people rightly fear it. In "No Name Woman," Maxine Hong Kingston ends the story by writing, "The Chinese are always very frightened of the drowned one, whose weeping ghost, wet hair hanging and skin bloated, waits silently by the water to pull down a substitute."* †

7) Like the miller, the hunter's wife is out of her mind with despair. It seems in this story that to receive the dubious help of magical characters the protagonists must be out of their minds.

8) Dreams had symbolic power long before our post-Freudian age. Messages come in dreams in many fairy tales. The notion that dreams reveal truths is an ancient one.

9) The full moon would have been bright indeed in times before light pollution. The soft illumination of the moon glinting on the golden comb of a beautiful young woman would have made her especially alluring. The hunter would yearn for his bride at the very sight of her.

the mill-pond she guessed at once what had befallen him. She was nearly beside herself with grief, and roamed round and round the pond calling on her husband without ceasing.[7] At last, worn out with sorrow and fatigue, she fell asleep and dreamt that she was wandering along a flowery meadow, when she came to a hut where she found an old witch, who promised to restore her husband to her.

When she awoke next morning she determined to set out and find the witch; so she wandered on for many a day, and at last she reached the flowery meadow and found the hut where the old witch lived. The poor wife told her all that had happened and how she had been told in a dream of the witch's power to help her.[8]

The witch counseled her to go to the pond the first time there was a full moon, and to comb her black hair with a golden comb, and then to place the comb on the bank. The hunter's wife gave the witch a handsome present, thanked her heartily, and returned home.

Time dragged heavily till the time of the full moon, but it passed at last, and as soon as it rose the young wife went to the pond, combed her black hair with a golden comb, and when she had finished, placed the comb on the bank; then she watched the water impatiently.[9] Soon she heard a rushing sound, and a big wave rose suddenly and swept the comb off the bank, and a minute after the head of her husband rose from the pond and gazed sadly at her.[10] But immediately another wave came, and the head sank back into the water without having said a word. The pond lay still and motionless, glittering in the moonshine, and the hunter's wife was not a bit better off than she had been before.

In despair she wandered about for days and nights, and at last, worn out by fatigue, she sank once more into a deep sleep, and dreamt exactly the same dream about the old witch. So next morning she went again to the flowery meadow and sought the witch in her hut, and told her of her grief. The old woman counseled her to go to the mill-pond the next full moon and play upon a golden flute, and then to lay the flute on the bank.[11]

As soon as the next moon was full the hunter's wife went to the mill-pond, played on a golden flute, and when she had finished placed it on the bank. Then a rushing sound was heard, and a wave swept the flute off the bank, and soon the head of the hunter appeared and rose up higher and higher till he was half out of the water. Then he gazed sadly at his wife and stretched out his arms towards her.

10) Although the disappearance of the hunter might be read as a poorly disguised example of infidelity, his emotion here suggests that he is entirely unwilling to be parted from his wife.

11) Music hath charms. Much like the comb, the golden flute would shine richly in the moonlight, and its music would lure a man from the water. But not this man. Try as I might, I am not sure why the hunter is first heads above the water, then shoulders above, then all the way out of the water. Unless it is nothing more than the usual rule of three events or tools in fairy tales.

12) A symbol of female
activity and
industriousness for
hundreds of years, the
spinning wheel provides
a powerful image of how
useful the hunter's wife
can be.

13) The threat of drowning
appears again, plus the
flood would evoke the
Biblical story of Noah
and the flood.

But another rushing wave arose and dragged him under once more. The hunter's wife, who had stood on the bank full of joy and hope, sank into despair when she saw her husband snatched away again before her eyes.

But for her comfort she dreamt the same dream a third time, and betook herself once more to the old witch's hut in the flowery meadow. This time the old woman told her to go the next full moon to the mill-pond, and to spin there with a golden spinning-wheel, and then to leave the spinning-wheel on the bank.[12]

The hunter's wife did as she was advised, and the first night the moon was full she sat and spun with a golden spinning-wheel, and then left the wheel on the bank. In a few minutes a rushing sound was heard in the waters, and a wave swept the spinning-wheel from the bank. Immediately the head of the hunter rose up from the pond, getting higher and higher each moment, till at length he stepped on to the bank and fell on his wife's neck.

But the waters of the pond rose up suddenly, overflowed the bank where the couple stood, and dragged them under the flood.[13] In her despair the young wife called on the old witch to help her, and in a moment the hunter was turned into a frog and his wife into a toad.[14] But they were not able to remain together, for the water tore them apart, and when the flood was over they both resumed their own shapes again, but the hunter and the hunter's wife found themselves each in a strange country, and neither knew what had become of the other.

The hunter determined to become a shepherd, and his wife too became a shepherdess. So they herded their sheep for many years in solitude and sadness.[15]

Now it happened once that the shepherd came to the country where the shepherdess lived. The neighborhood pleased him, and he saw that the pasture was rich and suitable for his flocks. So he brought his sheep there, and herded them as before. The shepherd and shepherdess became great friends, but they did not recognize each other in the least.[16]

But one evening when the moon was full they sat together watching their flocks, and the shepherd played upon his flute. Then the shepherdess thought of that evening when she had sat at the full moon by the mill-pond and had played on the golden flute; the recollection was too much for her, and she burst into tears. The shepherd asked her why she was crying, and left her no peace till she told him all her story. Then the scales fell from the

14) *Interesting. They are turned into amphibians. The hunter once dwelled under water and, now, both he and his wife are briefly animals that dwell in water and on land.*

15) *Shepherding is a notably lonely occupation. The storyteller would hardly have needed to point out the solitude of the couple to pre-modern audiences.*

16) *This is a twist that makes "The Nixy" a truly unusual fairy tale. The characters age and grow in the story—separately, yet side by side.*

17) Like Saul on the road to Damascus, the hero can at last see as he needs to. The word "scales," might also playfully refer to the fact that he once lived under water.

shepherd's eyes, and he recognized his wife, and she him.[17] So they returned joyfully to their own home, and lived in peace and happiness ever after.

Source Note

† Kingston, Maxine Hong. "No Name Woman." In *Literacies: Reading, Writing, Interpretation*, edited by Terence Brunk et al, 323-33. 2nd ed. New York: W.W. Norton, 2000. 333.

THE SOLDIER AND THE VAMPIRE

Introduction

"The Soldier and the Vampire" doesn't seem like a fairy tale at first glance. In fact, it may barely qualify. But this story does have a sorcerer, a hero, darkly magical activity, and a happy ending. So into *Beyond the Glass Slipper* it went. The emotional appeal of the story lies in the soldier's clear sense of purpose, his lack of fear, and his strong loyalties. The details of death, fire, sorcery, blood draining, and a wedding make it an imaginative delight.

Ghosts and monsters can be found in fairy tales. Cannibalism certainly is. Just think of "Hansel and Gretel," and "Snow White." "The Soldier and the Vampire" lures audiences into a dark night, in the middle of a lonely stretch in the Land of the Czars. Think of the leaping fires, the cold night air. The warning the miller gives to the hero: avoid the night. An evil man has died and has come back from the dead. The whole story could have been the basis for a Universal monster movie from the 1940s.

The soldier, however, has a stout heart and is armed with his faith in God and Emperor. Whether his constant belief is appealing to audiences on the personal level or not, it's clear that his beliefs sustain him through the terrible night he faces. He's a comforting figure in that he's predictable. He's also polite and friendly and physically brave. He's an action hero fashioned before action heroes existed in Hollywood. That he comes from dark, cold, exotic Russia, as vast and mysterious a country as any on Earth, gives him further appeal to Westernized audiences, who tend to think classic fairy tales must be set in quaint French and German locales. Or under the sea. Or in Hollywood's conception of the "Middle East."

The other half of the team, the vampire, is most intriguing when he's been broken into his disgusting parts. Reptiles and maggots and crow—oh my! Corralling his disgusting bits is a communal event, much like the wedding the vampire ruined the night before. Only instead of dancing and drinking, there's burning at the stake and sweeping up. The scene puts one in mind of the movie *Frankenstein* (1931), when the villagers burn down a windmill with the monster in it.

"The Soldier and the Vampire" provides its audience with enough detail to inspire our imaginations. In that sense it is truly a tale of wonder and transformation, as we see a simple man morph into a vampire-slaying hero. A hero who just wants to go home, get some sleep, and see his family.

Consider:

- Fearing both God and the adept in magic is common in fairy tales. One need only read "Hansel and Gretel" to see the power a witch can have in the minds of early fairy tale audiences. Look at "The Little Mermaid" to see how exacting God is said to be. The Mermaid is expected to work for 300 years to gain a soul—*after* having suffered numerous tortures in the name of love and in the quest for a soul. Entities with power are almost always intimidating in fairy tales, whether king or witch or deity. Does the fear of powerful but "godless" creatures in fairy tales suggest a lingering belief in old gods and spirits? Doesn't their intimidating power suggest a near-equality to God that undermines proclaimed belief in an all-powerful, single deity? Does the intense power found in sorcerers, witches, fairies, dwarfs, etc., suggest a lack of faith in the power of the God that fairy tale characters often proclaim to have? What explains this?

- The degree to which the soldier upholds the values of the state and the emperor (czar) is notable in this tale. "The Soldier and the Vampire," provides a useful path for investigating how different societies adapt or invent fairy tales to fit their social order. The czar and the people and the state were viewed as one. Contrast this tale with say, "Puss in Boots," in which a miller's son can rather easily become noble, through almost no effort of his own. In this tale, the soldier ends up well off, but he also finishes his stint in the army first. He does not leave his appointed station.

- The soldier proclaims his unity with the czar and state, saying, "I serve God and the Emperor." The soldier's statement reminds the audience of the distinctions between the vampire, who is revealed to be made of numerous foul parts, and the soldier, who is part of a great whole. How does the integrity of the "good" whole in this story versus the pieces of the corrupt differ from other tales? Is this tale an outlier in this regard? Can you find a cognate?

- Like stories in which the hero must survive a night in a haunted house, the soldier is delivered from the torments of the night by the light of dawn. As a vampiric entity, the dead sorcerer cannot survive the cleansing fire of the day's new light. The goodness of light and the uncertainty and danger of darkness is a powerful theme in fairy tales. Could this be the result of the nighttime having once been (literally) much more dangerous than now? Nighttime can be more dangerous than daytime in the twenty-first century, yet the distinction is not nearly as serious as it once was. Why do stories about surviving until light comes still captivate us? Are there fears that old stories address that will resonate no matter how everyday life changes?

- What's the after story for our soldier? Does he become a vampire killer? Does he marry and have a passel of children? Does the vampire somehow reorganize, like all self-respecting creatures of the night? How would you continue the story?

THE SOLDIER AND THE VAMPIRE

(From *Russian Folk-Tales*, by W.R. S. Ralston, 1873)

A certain soldier was allowed to go home on furlough.[1] Well, he walked and walked, and after a time he began to draw near to his native village. Not far off from that village lived a miller in his mill. In old times the soldier had been very intimate with him: why shouldn't he go and see his friend? He went. The miller[2] received him cordially, and at once brought out liquor; and the two began drinking, and chattering about their ways and doings.[3] All this took place towards nightfall, and the soldier stopped so long at the miller's that it grew quite dark.

When he proposed to start for his village, his host exclaimed:

"Spend the night here, trooper! It's very late now, and perhaps you might run into mischief."

"How so?"

"God is punishing us! A terrible warlock has died among us, and by night he rises from his grave, wanders through the village, and does such things as bring fear upon the very boldest! How could even you help being afraid of him?"

1) The word "certain" gives a sense of specificity that raises the notion that the name of someone the listeners know could be inserted here, giving the story a pleasing sense of realism.

2) The miller, like the soldier, is a stock character in fairy tales. Millers were often fairly well off as well, so receiving hospitality from a miller would be a detail that rings true.

3) The sense of conviviality here, almost of two old friends drinking and laughing, will make what comes next seem more macabre than it otherwise would have.

4) Google sleuthing did little for me on the saying.

(cont.) Justriddlesandmore.com suggests the saying is a riddle and the answer is "ice." It's entirely possible that it is a play on a riddle, but possibly, it's a way to acknowledge the absolute power of the czar in Russia. Like ice, he is a force that cannot be easily broken. The czar's power is dense and solid. Of Ivan the Terrible, Martin Sixsmith writes, "All men outside the Church, including the nobility, were bound to lifelong service to the state; conscription was a universal duty, and the tsar's authority in all matters was absolute."†

5) *Sewing the boots seems to have a touch of foreshadowing. I found myself wondering if they signified that the vampire would go on a journey.*

6) *The soldier is forthrightly nosy here. The vampire seems to be changing the subject by asking him to a wedding, an invitation likely to make the soldier fall in with the vampire's plans.*

7) *A wedding has several potential symbolic messages here. First, it would be a big, community event. Second,*

"Not a bit of it! A soldier is a man who belongs to the crown, and 'crown property cannot be drowned in water nor burnt in fire.'[4] I'll be off: I'm tremendously anxious to see my people as soon as possible."

Off he set. His road lay in front of a graveyard. On one of the graves he saw a great fire blazing. "What's that?" thinks he. "Let's have a look." When he drew near, he saw that the warlock was sitting by the fire, sewing boots.[5]

"Hail, brother!" calls out the soldier.

The warlock looked up and said:

"What have you come here for?"

"Why, I wanted to see what you're doing."

The warlock threw his work aside and invited the soldier to a wedding.

"Come along, brother," says he, "let's enjoy ourselves. There's a wedding going on in the village."[6]

"Come along!" says the soldier.

They came to where the wedding was; there they were given drink, and treated with the utmost hospitality.[7] The warlock drank and drank, reveled and reveled, and then grew angry. He chased all the guests and relatives out of the house, threw the wedded pair into a slumber, took out two phials and an awl, pierced the hands of the bride and bridegroom with the awl, and began drawing off their blood.[8] Having done this, he said to the soldier:

"Now let's be off."

Well, they went off.

On the way the soldier said:

"Tell me; why did you draw off their blood in those phials?"

"Why, in order that the bride and bridegroom might die. Tomorrow morning no one will be able to wake them. I alone know how to bring them back to life."[9]

"How's that managed?"

"The bride and bridegroom must have cuts made in their heels, and some of their own blood must then be poured back into those wounds. I've got the bridegroom's blood stowed away in my right-hand pocket, and the bride's in my left."

The soldier listened to this without letting a single word escape him. Then the warlock began boasting again.

"Whatever I wish," says he, "That I can do!"

"I suppose it's quite impossible to get the better of you?" says the soldier.

"Why impossible? If any one were to make a pyre of aspen boughs, a hundred loads of them, and were to burn me on that pyre, then he'd be able

(cont.) hospitality even to strangers like the soldier and the vampire would be expected. Third, the alcohol served at such an event loosens people up. Fourth, the bride and groom symbolize young, innocent people at the very start of life, in great contrast to the vampire.

8) *The vampire is now an angry, violent drunk. A drunk at any wedding is a scourge—the stuff of wedding nightmares, but the vampire is much more. He came for mischief and uses the awl to do terrible damage to the bridal couple. Note that an awl is used in leather work, and that this scene is probably what the shoemaking actually foreshadowed.*

9) *The widely-held view that vampires drink the blood of victims to sustain their own existence does not seem to apply in this story. The story suggests that the vampire here draws blood to cause misery and to gain power over the populace. In keeping with the Russian tradition that a sorcerer becomes a* heritik *after death, our*

(cont.) sorcerer is probably undead because of his lack of belief in God during his life. Heritiks face a variety of fates after death, a bloodsucker being only one of them. Sometimes they eat people.‡

10) Wheedling information out of villains is a time-honored tradition in fairy tales. Protagonists like soldiers and millers' sons are usually fairly straightforward, even simple-seeming men. But they can have cunning. Here, the soldier gets everything he needs to prevail from the vampire's mouth in what seems to be a reverse boast by the latter. The vampire scoffs at the impossibility of destroying him, but proceeds to detail the horrific components of his undead body. Evil creatures made of disgusting elements routinely shows up in horror and fantasy. One example is an episode from Buffy the Vampire Slayer, *"What's My Line, Part One?" in which one of the bad guys is composed of maggots. Memorable.* Buffy *often incorporated elements of myth, fairy tales, and folklore into episodes.*

11) Like stories in which the hero must survive a night in a haunted house, the soldier is

to get the better of me. Only he'd have to look out sharp in burning me; for snakes and worms and different kinds of reptiles would creep out of my inside, and crows and magpies and jackdaws would come flying up. All these must be caught and flung on the pyre. If so much as a single maggot were to escape, then there'd be no help for it; in that maggot I should slip away!"[10]

The soldier listened to all this and did not forget it. He and the warlock talked and talked, and at last they arrived at the grave.

"Well, brother," said the warlock, "now I'll tear you to pieces. Otherwise you'd be telling all this."

"What are you talking about? Don't you deceive yourself; I serve God and the Emperor."

The warlock gnashed his teeth, howled aloud, and sprang at the soldier—who drew his sword and began laying about him with sweeping blows. They struggled and struggled; the soldier was all but at the end of his strength. "Ah!" thinks he, "I'm a lost man—and all for nothing!" Suddenly the cocks began to crow. The warlock fell lifeless to the ground.[11]

The soldier took the phials of blood out of the warlock's pockets, and went on to the house of his own people. When he had got there, and had exchanged greetings with his relatives, they said: "Did you see any disturbance, soldier?"

"No, I saw none."[12]

"There now! Why we've a terrible piece of work going on in the village. A warlock has taken to haunting it!"

After talking awhile, they lay down to sleep. Next morning the soldier awoke, and began asking: "I'm told you've got a wedding going on somewhere here?"

"There was a wedding in the house of a rich moujik,"[13] replied his relative, "but the bride and bridegroom have died this very night—what from, nobody knows."

They showed him the house. Thither he went without speaking a word. When he got there, he found the whole family in tears.

"What are you mourning about?" says he.

"Such and such is the state of things soldier," say they.

"I can bring your young people to life again. What will you give me if I do?"

"Take what you like, even were it half of what we've got!"[14]

The soldier did as the warlock had instructed him, and brought the young

(cont.) delivered from the torments of the night by the light of dawn. As a vampiric entity, the dead sorcerer cannot survive the cleansing fire of the day's new light.

12) Why the soldier remains mum about the night's previous events is unclear, but doing so may increase his credibility as a hero. He keeps his own counsel, not spreading gossip that would further frighten the villagers. Or, perhaps more plausibly, he has already figured out that there is profit to be gained from his night with a vampire.

13) A Russian peasant.

14) Soldiering is seldom a profitable profession. Fortunately for him, like many a poor man of the road in fairy tales, the soldier is to be rewarded for his bravery and persistence. Note that unlike, say, Jack, from "Jack and the Beanstalk," the

(cont.) soldier is no thief who is unfairly rewarded with stolen riches.

15) *This detailed gross-out scene helps move this fairy tale into the horror genre, reminding present-day audiences that horror was not invented by modern-day movie makers. In addition, as a heretic in life, the dead warlock must be burned in death. Finally, by going to the starosta, who would be a kind of village leader, audiences are reminded that the soldier is a by-the-book kind of hero.*

16) *The last paragraph proves the soldier's dedication to the State. He might have found a way out of the military or perhaps risked it all through desertion. Instead, he meets his obligations, and, without blowing his money on riotous living, lives a fairly realistic-seeming happily ever after.*

people back to life. Instead of weeping there began to be happiness and rejoicing; the soldier was hospitably treated and well rewarded. Then—left about, face!—off he marched to the Starosta, and told him to call the peasants together and to get ready a hundred loads of aspen wood. Well, they took the wood into the graveyard, dragged the warlock out of his grave, placed him on the pyre, and set it alight—the people all standing round in a circle with brooms, shovels, and fire-irons. The pyre became wrapped in flames, the warlock began to burn. His corpse burst, and out of it crept snakes, worms, and all sorts of reptiles, and up came flying crows, magpies, and jackdaws. The peasants knocked them down and flung them into the fire, not allowing so much as a single maggot to creep away! And so the warlock was thoroughly consumed, and the soldier collected his ashes and strewed them to the winds. From that time forth there was peace in the village.[15]

The soldier received the thanks of the whole community. He stayed at home some time, enjoying himself thoroughly. Then he went back to the czar's service with money in his pocket. When he had served his time, he retired from the army, and began to live at his ease.[16]

Source Notes

† Oinas, Felix J. "Heretics As Vampires and Demons in Russia." *The Slavic and Eastern European Journal* 22, no. 4 (Winter 1978): 433-441.

‡ Sixsmith, Martin. *Russia: A 1,000 Year Chronicle of the Wild East.* New York, NY: Overlook Pr., 2012. 48.

THE THREE PENNIES

Introduction

"The Grateful Dead" isn't just an awesome, old, and largely defunct rock band, fronted by the late Jerry Garcia. It's a category of folklore that features ghosts getting help in finding eternal rest. As such, the stories probably more rightly belong to folklore rather than fairy tales, but I just could not resist. Besides, for the purposes of this book, wonder and transformation satisfy the requirements for inclusion, and the lines between fairy tale and folklore aren't always distinct to begin with. (This was how I rationalized using this story to myself. Clearly, opinions will differ.)

Stories like "The Three Pennies" feature human heroes who are humbly or nobly born, but no matter what their station, they are rewarded by an undead person for a simple act of kindness. By paying the grave robbers to leave a dead body alone, the soldier sets off a chain of events that leaves him in better circumstances by the end of the story.

A notable feature of the grateful dead stories is that they are, as far as I can tell, "buddy" or road stories of two guys, a live and a dead one, encountering adventures in which the ghost or revenant saves the day, and gradually improves the prospects of the hero. Details matter in all stories, but grateful dead tales seem to come alive especially well with action details of chases and danger that stimulates the imagination of anyone who reads or hears them. They are exciting. Two men are bound together by kindness and face terrible foes so a debt can be repaid. Cue the special effects.

As for the band, The Grateful Dead, the general opinion seems to be that they got the name from an encyclopedia or dictionary. The best explanation I have found (meaning the one I like the best) comes from the site *The Straight Dope: Fighting Ignorance Since 1973 (It's taking longer than we thought)*. In the explainer about the band's name, Cecil Adams (the brain behind *The Straight Dope*) notes that Garcia said he found the name in a dictionary. Adams then begins to spin an exciting, and to my thinking, utterly convincing near-theory that Garcia possibly found the term in the *Funk & Wagnall's Standard Dictionary of Folklore, Mythology and Legend*. Follow up, however, makes it clear that Garcia found the term in an old, run of the mill Funk & Wagnall's dictionary.

"The Three Pennies" has magic, a princess connected to a strange prophesy, a leaden ship, ghouls, a road trip, and two otherworldly creatures telling each other off. It's fun. As The Grateful Dead can be.

Consider:

- The rule of threes is one of the most common motifs that appear in fairy tales and folklore, and "The Three Pennies" takes the idea further than most stories. The number three is symbolically important in Christianity (the Trinity), and audiences in Denmark, where this tale is from, would readily, perhaps even subconsciously, understand this. Beyond Christianity, the number has importance in Buddhism, Judaism, and religions across the world.

  Three implements, three men to wield them, and three pennies not only invoke religious images, but remind readers and listeners of other tales, like "Snow White," when Snow is tempted three times by her stepmother in disguise. From early on, three makes the audience both comfortable and wanting more. Does the story fulfill the promise the idea of three suggests in the beginning? In what ways? Did new details change everything up and bring surprises?

- The villains give up easily. Why? Is it to pave the way for the story, which, as a fairy tale, is a relatively simple one? Or, could we trust that audiences were and are filling in blanks?

- The passage in which the ghost asks the soldier to smell the old woman's hair is one of the reasons I chose "The Three Pennies" for inclusion in this volume. It's simply bizarre. It makes me laugh, because it's as though the ghost is teasing the old soldier. Why smell the hair? What is this about? I look forward to any ideas from readers of this book. The sentence delights and mystifies me.

- The ghost and the conjurer get into a shouting match near the end of the story, in what is another delightfully weird scene. Why would the conjurer bother to stay and shout? Is he just a blowhard? The moment of the conjurer's destruction is one of several nods to well-known fairy tales in this story. In this case, it's "Rumpelstiltskin," who also destroys himself with rage. Flint is a hard substance that can be used to make fire—reminding audiences that sorcerers engage in the devil's work. That the Count is also a troll, as we learn in the next passage, makes his fate all the more fitting, considering that trolls are often portrayed negatively in fairy tales and folklore. References to other fairy tales are common in many such stories. What explains this? Is it a kind of storytelling shorthand? A form of salute or a tip of the hat, so to speak?

- What's the after story? Might the conjurer somehow reignite into a new trouble maker, from just one little piece of flint? Will our ghost friend rise again if our soldier hero is still in need? Do the soldier and his princess live happily ever after? If so, how?

THE THREE PENNIES

(From *Danish Fairy and Folk Tales*, by J. Christian Bay, 1899)

Many years ago an old soldier was discharged from the army. He received in consideration of his excellent and faithful service a small loaf of rye bread and three pennies, whereupon he was at liberty to go whither he pleased. As he was walking along the highroad, he met three men. The one carried a shovel, the second a pickaxe, and the third a spade.

The soldier stopped, looked at them, and said, "Where are you going?"

"I will tell you," answered one of them. "Today there was buried a man who owed each of us one penny, and now we will dig him up, since we are determined upon getting our dues."

"What an idea!" returned the soldier. "You had better leave the dead man alone. At any rate, he is at present unable to pay you even one penny, so don't disturb his peace!"[1]

"It is all very fine for you to talk," answered the man. "But we must have the money, and up he must come."

When the soldier felt that his fair words

1) As in the story "The Soldier and the Vampire," our hero is a righteous and straightforward fellow, who is shocked at the idea of disturbing the dead. In this way, he could be seen as speaking for the authority of the church and state. The delicious gruesomeness of disturbing the dead in order to get a small amount of money would serve to further entertain the audience. In a grateful dead story, something has to happen to make eternal rest impossible for the dead person in question.

2) With this line, we know that not only do we consider the three diggers ghouls, the soldier does as well. Ghouls are usually defined as grave robbers or even those who dine on the flesh of dead humans. Clearly, our three would-be diggers are in the former category.

3) The revenant is a purposeful ghost, sometimes a zombie. In this case, while our ghost has a mission, it clearly means well. While pale, he behaves as a human, and there is nothing scary about him.

4) This passage is intriguing. As the ghost is undead, it would seem that he shouldn't be able to go into a sacred space. Yet, he wants to, and the soldier refuses "wistfully." "Wistful," as in a little sad and yearning. Is the soldier sad for the ghost? Has the soldier another reason for not wanting to go in?

could not settle the matter, he said, "Here, I have two pennies. Will you take them and promise to leave the dead man undisturbed?"

"Two pennies are not to be refused," said the man again, "but they will pay only two of us. What can you give the third one, since he is bent upon having his share?"

As the soldier saw that there was no dealing with these three wretches, he resumed, "Since you are so desperately determined, here is my third and last penny. Take it, and be content."[2]

Now all three were well satisfied, so they pursued their way with the three pennies in their pockets.

When the soldier had advanced a distance, a stranger came walking along. He looked rather pale, but saluted the soldier in a very civil manner, and followed him along the road without uttering a single sound.[3]

At last they reached a church, and here the stranger turned to his companion, saying, "Let us walk in!"

The soldier looked wistfully at him, and answered, "That would not do. What business have we in the church at midnight?"[4]

"I tell you," replied the stranger, "we must walk in!"

Upon this they entered the church and walked straight up to the altar. There was an old woman sitting with a burning light in her hand.[5]

"Take a hair from her head, and smell at it!" commanded the stranger.[6]

The soldier complied, but nothing remarkable happened. The stranger asked him to repeat the action, which he did; but there was no effect. The third time, however, when he tore a whole tuft of hair from the woman's head, she became so furious that she darted off, out above the church, carrying the whole leaden vault with her.[7]

The two men went out of the church and down to the beach, where they found the whole leaden vault. Turning to the soldier, the stranger said, "Sit up. We will put to sea!"[8]

"Is that so?" remarked the soldier, who understood nothing of all this. "I see no ship, however."

"Let me manage it all," says the stranger. "Just seat yourself by me on the vault! Beyond the sea there is a princess of whom it was predicted that she would be married only to a man who should come across the sea in a leaden ship. Here you will be able to make your fortune."[9]

5) An old woman standing near treasure or an important tool is common in fairy tales. In Hans Christian Andersen's "The Tinderbox," an old witch greets the soldier and tells him about a hollow tree with untold treasure at the bottom. In this story, however, the old woman is strangely silent. As for the light, it may simply represent tapers to be found in churches the world over.

6) Possessing someone's hair was thought to capture some of his or her essence in witchcraft lore. Yet, despite the three attempts made by the soldier, the witch escapes with the vault the ghost seeks.

7) A leaden vault to hold the dead was common in small, old churches. What is not clear in this story is why the ghost is after the vault. Presumably, he seeks a burial place, but he does not make that intention clear. Or, perhaps he is planning the soldier's fate, even now.

8) That the vehicle he uses to cross the water ought to, by the laws of nature, sink to the bottom, suggests that powerful forces, embodied by the ghost, are arrayed on his side. At this point, it is clear that the soldier will have a happy ending to his story. The remaining fun is in the details.

9) *The prophecy of the princess marrying a man who comes to her in a leaden boat is in keeping with stories about sleeping beauties behind deadly briars, princesses set upon glass mountains, and girls locked away in impenetrable fortresses and towers. The soldier has already proven himself kindly and brave, but his work is not done. He must take a journey as strange as the one he already is on.*

10) *In many stories, the hero will need to fight more aggressively for the maiden, but this tale suddenly takes on some of the contours of "Puss in Boots," with the ghostly stranger tricking and battling a powerful sorcerer, in order to gain wealth for his companion.*

The leaden vault now floated out upon the open sea, and landed them safely on the other side. Great was the joy and happiness throughout the country, and the marriage between the soldier and the princess was celebrated with such pomp and splendor as was never seen, before or after.[10]

When the ceremony had been performed, and the carriage was standing in front of the church door, bride and groom entered, with the stranger who had followed the soldier all along. The coachman asked to what place he might drive them.

"Drive away, as fast as you can, towards the side where the sun will rise," said the stranger, and in a little while they were carried along at a furious rate.

Somewhere they saw a large herd of cattle. They stopped, and the soldier called the herdsman to the carriage door, asking who he was. "I am the Count of Ravensburg," answered the shepherd, "and yonder is my castle."

The stranger again bid the coachman drive as fast as possible. In a little while they rushed up to Ravensburg Castle. As they were ready to alight from the carriage, there was someone who knocked hard at the gate. It was the herdsman, who was anxious to come in. The stranger walked to the gate, inquiring what he could do for him. He wished to come into the castle, he said, for it belonged to him, and he had a right to demand admittance. The stranger meditated a little, whereupon he told the herdsman, who was a conjurer, that he might be allowed to come in, but first he must suffer the whole fate of the rye.[11]

"The fate of the rye!" repeated the conjurer. "What do you mean by that?"

"I mean," answered the stranger, "that next fall you must be sown deep in the ground, and towards spring, when you come up, you must ripen in the sunshine and grow in the rain until you are ready for the harvest. Then you will be mowed and dried, and kept in the barn, until at length you will be threshed."

"How is that!" cried the conjurer. "Am I to be threshed?"

"Of course you are," replied the stranger. "First you will be threshed, and then taken to the mill and ground."

"Ground, too!" shouted the conjurer. "Will I be ground also?"

"Yes, both ground and sifted," answered the stranger.

But the conjurer, hearing this, became so furious that he burst all into flint-stones.

The stranger now bid good-bye to the princess and the soldier, shook hands with them, and said, "Now I have seen you married to the princess. The troll of Ravensburg is dead and gone, and his

11) *Why a conjurer is herding cattle is never made clear. What is certain is that audiences would have known how rye is ground, so the details of the conjurer's fate would seem deliciously horrific. Grind his bones to make bread indeed. Another echo of another fairy tale. In this case "Jack in the Beanstalk."*

12) *Simple kindness, with no expectation of reward is what wins the soldier everything a man could wish for. The ghost feels his debt is repaid, and now he can move on. All has been made right. Does this pleasing simplicity ring true? Or, is this an example of the major complaint about fairy tales—that they are falsely simplistic and optimistic?*

castle, with all its treasures, is yours. I was as good to you as you were to me when you gave away your three pennies for my sake!"

"What do you say?" exclaimed the soldier. "I never thought of those three pennies again!"

"I know that," answered the stranger, "and otherwise I would not have been able to help you. However, I bid farewell to you and your wife, for I must return to the place where I belong."[12]

FAIRY GIFTS

Introduction

"Fairy Gifts," by Comte de Caylus, is the most overtly didactic story in *Beyond the Glass Slipper*, which is quite an achievement considering how much moralizing is found in fairy tales in general. The entire structure of the tale is built around an instructional program designed by the Flower Fairy, a powerful, benevolent deity who presides over an Edenic estate. Written by Comte de Caylus, who was better known as an antiquarian and artist than as an author of literary fairy tales, the story may have survived in English thanks to Andrew Lang including it in his *Green Fairy Book*, from 1892.

The style of "Fairy Gifts" is dense, wordy even, but that could be an effect of the translation of French into English. Or, it could be the formal style of writing employed by literary fairy tale writers of de Caylus's time. For example, the best-known version of "Beauty and the Beast," by Jeanne-Marie Le Prince de Beaumont, is heavier in description of setting and emotion than what we find in, say, "The Dirty Shepherdess," also in *Beyond the Glass Slipper*. At any rate, de Caylus and de Beaumont were rough contemporaries whose stories were not meant to reflect the oral tale-telling style of the common folk.

Princess Sylvia, the heroine of this story, is sent by the Flower

Fairy to visit four princesses whom the fairy raised and sent into the world. The fairy wants to bestow the very best gift to enhance Sylvia's personal charms. Each gift she made to the four older princesses embodies too much of a good thing: Princess Iris is too pretty, Daphne is too talkative, Cynthia too eager-to-please (especially men), and Phyllida's wit proves too sharp. Eventually, Princess Sylvia asks for a "quiet spirit," which appears to be serenity.

Moralizing to and about women is an integral part of fairy tale messaging. Feminist scholars have found rich ground in stories like "The Red Shoes" and "Snow White" to examine prohibitions against female vanity, for example. Yet, as is often the case with fairy tales, annoying preachiness is based in a solid truth about human behavior: excess in anything is dangerous, and faults like vanity, constant talking, being too eager-to-please, and caustic wit are to be deplored, in both men and women.

That basic truth about troublesome excess in manner or personality in "Fairy Gifts" helped make it a part of *Beyond the Glass Slipper*. Its direct, if wordy tone (there's a touch of Princess Daphne in de Caylus, perhaps) makes it easy to understand in terms of overall message. Its detail about the faults of the four princesses gives audiences plenty to think over.

Consider:

- Is the story designed to call to mind the Garden of Eden, from the Old Testament? If so, is there a fall? Or, does the story assume an after-the-fall scenario? The author takes some pains to describe just how perfect the Flower Fairy's garden is, with its gorgeous plants and ponds and the general perfect happiness of its lucky inhabitants. Is it more likely that the Flower Fairy's court is meant to symbolize the way adults recall childhood: simpler, dreamier and easier than, in fact, it often actually was?

- Are the names of the princesses, including Sylvia, significant? (The traditional meanings of names are easy to find.) The Flower Fairy is given no special name of her own, yet Sylvia and the other four princesses are designated? Why is that?

- Fairy tales often warn us against wanting the wrong things. The stepmother in "Snow White" wants to be the most beautiful woman in the kingdom after she has begun to age. The miller in "The Nixy" wants relief from his financial woes so much that he is willing to make a bargain with a water spirit. The wife in "Rapunzel" wants rampion so much (and her husband so wants to please her) that he sneaks into the garden of a powerful witch to steal it. Also, in "Fairy Gifts," Iris, Daphne, Cynthia, and Phyllida have, based on the information the story gives us, asked for and received great beauty, charm, eloquence, and wit, but it has brought them no great joy. They all wanted gifts that would make them superior to others in a significant area. In short, they wanted gifts that externally impress, rather than the gift Sylvia asked for, which was about internal peace. Considering other fairy tales, can you find one or two that have a message about the importance of internal peace and fortitude of the spirit? If so, which ones, and how are they like and unlike "Fairy Gifts"?

- "Fairy Gifts" is unlike many fairy tales in that it actually features a fairy. Some fairy tales have witches and sorcerers, magical objects and animal helpers, but no actual fairies. Could it represent a transitional meaning or alternative meaning for how we currently view "fairies"—as glittery old godmothers or otherworldly sticklike creatures who flit about largely ignoring us? Or could it be that stories about fairies became conflated with myths, legends and fables over the years (especially after the advent of films and television)? Does it matter or not matter?

- As with the other tales in this book, what kind of after story would you give "Fairy Gifts"? What would Sylvia's life be like? What about the other princesses? Do they ever get any peace or anything resembling happiness? Does the fairy have a back story or an origin story? Any potential romances or families for these characters?

FAIRY GIFTS

(From Andrew Lang's *The Green Fairy Book*, 1892)

It generally happens that people's surroundings reflect more or less accurately their minds and dispositions, so perhaps that is why the Flower Fairy lived in a lovely palace, with the most delightful garden you can imagine, full of flowers, and trees, and fountains, and fish-ponds, and everything nice.[1] For the Fairy herself was so kind and charming that everybody loved her, and all the young princes and princesses who formed her court were as happy as the day was long, simply because they were near her.[2] They came to her when they were quite tiny, and never left her until they were grown up and had to go away into the great world; and when that time came she gave to each whatever gift he asked of her.[3] But it is chiefly of the Princess Sylvia that you are going to hear now. The Fairy loved her with all her heart, for she was at once original and gentle, and

1) *Flowers are ephemeral, associated with feminine youthful beauty and fertility, which may be why they are so prominent in this description. On a completely different note, this is a remarkably classist opening. Do people who are forced to live in squalor and poverty have naturally poor and disordered brains? Or perhaps I am applying twenty-first century attitudes where they don't fit.*

2) *De Caylus has offered a perfect childhood for our heroine. One we would all like to have had. The Flower Fairy is like a benevolent deity, creating a perfect world in which to grow and, well, flower.*

3) *Her excellent nature and character established, what the Flower Fairy does is worth noting and possibly emulating. She is quite the maternal figure: wise, generous and providing a gorgeous environment in which her charges can grow.*

she had nearly reached the age at which the gifts were generally bestowed.[4] However, the Fairy had a great wish to know how the other princesses who had grown up and left her were prospering, and before the time came for Sylvia to go herself, she resolved to send her to some of them. So one day her chariot, drawn by butterflies, was made ready, and the Fairy said: "Sylvia, I am going to send you to the court of Iris; she will receive you with pleasure for my sake as well as for your own. In two months you may come back to me again, and I shall expect you to tell me what you think of her."[5]

Sylvia was very unwilling to go away, but as the Fairy wished it she said nothing—only when the two months were over she stepped joyfully into the butterfly chariot, and could not get back quickly enough to the Flower Fairy, who, for her part, was equally delighted to see her again.[6]

"Now, child," said she, "tell me what impression you have received."

"You sent me, madam," answered Sylvia, "to the Court of Iris, on whom you had bestowed the gift of beauty. She never tells anyone, however, that it was your gift, though she often speaks of your kindness in general. It seemed to me that her loveliness, which fairly dazzled me at first, had absolutely deprived her of the use of any of her other gifts or graces. In allowing herself to be seen, she appeared to think that she was doing all that could possibly be required of her. But, unfortunately, while I was still with her she became seriously ill, and though she presently recovered, her beauty is entirely gone, so that she hates the very sight of herself, and is in despair. She entreated me to tell you what had happened, and to beg you, in pity, to give her beauty back to her. And, indeed, she does need it terribly, for all the things in her that were tolerable, and even agreeable, when she was so pretty, seem quite different now she is ugly, and it is so long since she thought of using her mind or her natural cleverness, that I really don't think she has any left now. She is quite aware of all this herself, so you may imagine how unhappy she is, and how earnestly she begs for your aid."[7]

"You have told me what I wanted to know," cried the Fairy, "but alas! I cannot help her; my gifts can be given but once."

(cont.) action. The little mermaid ignores her grandmother's admonitions to forget about the world above. Snow White opens the door to the woman the dwarfs have warned her against. Cinderella proves herself adept at deceiving her stepsisters and her stepmother. Sylvia, however, is perfectly obedient.

7) The push and pull of the beauty question in fairy tales is evident here. While prettiness is usually equated with goodness of character, the sin of vanity is also spotlighted. Consider "The Girl Who Trod on the Loaf," by Hans Christian Andersen. Ingrid, the main character, is a beautiful, but terribly vain little girl, who ends up a statue in Hell's waiting room because of her overwhelming pride in appearance. Yet for all the annoying moral preachiness of fairy tales, the foolishness of relying on something as ephemeral as beauty is hard to argue about. Beauty inevitably does fade in both men and women, but the ability to be a good companion matters at all ages.

8) *Women who talk too much are given a pretty hard time in fairy tales. Yet, this story is entirely woman-focused and takes women very seriously as people and as leaders of royal courts. Women are in charge, women are the actors, women are the point of this story. They matter. Besides, foolish talk by men is deplored in fairy tales and folklore as well. See the miller in "Rumpelstiltskin." One false boast about his daughter and trouble ensues.*

Some time passed in all the usual delights of the Flower Fairy's palace, and then she sent for Sylvia again, and told her she was to stay for a little while with the Princess Daphne, and accordingly the butterflies whisked her off, and set her down in quite a strange kingdom. But she had only been there a very little time before a wandering butterfly brought a message from her to the Fairy, begging that she might be sent for as soon as possible, and before very long she was allowed to return.

"Ah! Madam," cried she, "what a place you sent me to that time!"

"Why, what was the matter?" asked the Fairy. "Daphne was one of the princesses who asked for the gift of eloquence, if I remember rightly."

"And very ill the gift of eloquence becomes a woman," replied Sylvia, with an air of conviction. "It is true that she speaks well, and her expressions are well chosen; but then she never leaves off talking, and though at first one may be amused, one ends by being wearied to death. Above all things she loves any assembly for settling the affairs of her kingdom, for on those occasions she can talk and talk without fear of interruption; but, even then, the moment it is over she is ready to begin again about anything or nothing, as the case may be. Oh! How glad I was to come away I cannot tell you."[8]

The Fairy smiled at Sylvia's unfeigned disgust at her late experience; but after allowing her a little time to recover she sent her to the Court of the Princess Cynthia, where she left her for three months. At the end of that time Sylvia came back to her with all the joy and contentment that one feels at being once more beside a dear friend. The Fairy, as usual, was anxious to hear what she thought of Cynthia, who had always been amiable, and to whom she had given the gift of pleasing.

"I thought at first," said Sylvia, "that she must be the happiest Princess in the world; she had a thousand lovers who vied with one another in their efforts to please and gratify her. Indeed, I had nearly decided that I would ask a similar gift."

"Have you altered your mind, then?" interrupted the Fairy.

"Yes, indeed, madam," replied Sylvia; "and I will tell you why. The longer I stayed the more I saw that Cynthia was not really happy. In her desire to please everyone she ceased to be sincere, and degenerated into a mere coquette; and even her lovers felt that the charms and fascinations which were exercised upon all who approached her without distinction were valueless, so that in the end they ceased to care for them, and went away disdainfully."[9]

"I am pleased with you, child" said the

9) *Princes Cynthia illustrates the perils of being too eager-to-please. Everyone likes easygoing, undemanding people, but most of us want a challenge in friends and lovers. Like the other princesses who serve to warn Sylvia, Cynthia is an example of too much of a good thing. She is called a "coquette," which usually means a woman who flirts with men without thought or discernment. Yet Cynthia's desire to please goes beyond romance and seems to take in everyone she meets, with no sense of reserve or dignity.*

10) *The desire to score conversational points can be the downfall of quick-thinking and witty talkers. Savage wit can be charming, but sooner or later, it dawns on listeners that a needling wit can easily be turned on them. Once again, the dissatisfaction Sylvia experiences is based on degree. Sparkling repartee is exciting—until it becomes exhausting.*

Fairy; "enjoy yourself here for awhile and presently you shall go to Phyllida."

Sylvia was glad to have leisure to think, for she could not make up her mind at all what she should ask for herself, and the time was drawing very near. However, before very long the Fairy sent her to Phyllida, and waited for her report with unabated interest.

"I reached her court safely," said Sylvia, "and she received me with much kindness, and immediately began to exercise upon me that brilliant wit which you had bestowed upon her. I confess that I was fascinated by it, and for a week thought that nothing could be more desirable; the time passed like magic, so great was the charm of her society. But I ended by ceasing to covet that gift more than any of the others I have seen, for, like the gift of pleasing, it cannot really give satisfaction. By degrees I wearied of what had so delighted me at first, especially as I perceived more and more plainly that it is impossible to be constantly smart and amusing without being frequently ill-natured, and too apt to turn all things, even the most serious, into mere occasions for a brilliant jest."[10]

The Fairy in her heart agreed with Sylvia's conclusions, and felt pleased with herself for having brought her up so well.

But now the time was come for Sylvia to

receive her gift, and all her companions were assembled; the Fairy stood in the midst and in the usual manner asked what she would take with her into the great world.

Sylvia paused for a moment, and then answered: "A quiet spirit." And the Fairy granted her request.

This lovely gift makes life a constant happiness to its possessor, and to all who are brought into contact with her. She has all the beauty of gentleness and contentment in her sweet face; and if at times it seems less lovely through some chance grief or disquietude, the hardest thing that one ever hears said is:

"Sylvia's dear face is pale to-day. It grieves one to see her so."

And when, on the contrary, she is gay and joyful, the sunshine of her presence rejoices all who have the happiness of being near her.[11]

11) *A serene spirit is what most of us want: Calm, accepting of life's challenges—easy going, but not a pushover. In terms of Sylvia's personal development, "The Fairy Gifts" represents a genuine happily ever after. Also, while the Flower Fairy does bestow Sylvia's gift, the request came from an earned awareness on Sylvia's part about the qualities that make a person content.*

THE LOVING PAIR

Introduction

Hans Christian Andersen's fairy tales were specifically written for children as a first audience. But like most great children's stories, his tales were meant to entertain readers of all ages. "The Loving Pair" focuses on one of Andersen's favorite themes: the confusion romantic love brings to the people who feel it.

On the surface, this story is very much for children. Part of the action takes place in the nursery. The two halves of the couple are toys who can talk to each other. The action of the tale involves spinning and bouncing. Yet the conversation in the story is all about appearances and unrequited love and the inability most people have to see beyond the surface—messages that resonate with people of all ages. In addition, his fairly overt suggestions about the power of appearance and social class as influences on romantic love clearly speak to adults.

Andersen was famously a class traveler. The child of a shoemaker in Odense, Denmark, he grew up poor, but as long as his father was alive, Andersen had a happy childhood, filled with love and strong encouragement from his father, who valued young Hans's creativity. When Andersen was 11, his father died and the youngster had to work to help feed his family. It took many years for Andersen to get the education and advantages he wanted, and eventually, he became world famous. He adored fame and fortune and shamelessly enjoyed being with the rich and powerful. Yet, because of his bad luck in romance and the class prejudices of his time, Andersen never felt fully accepted by other people. He always saw himself as an outsider and never forgot what it was like to be rejected romantically and socially. His stories reflect that perspective.

"The Loving Pair" was chosen for inclusion in *Beyond the Glass Slipper* because it encapsulates some of Andersen's best traits as a writer: effective social commentary, skillfully rendered description, and a willingness to write sad endings to his tales for children. While the story does read as preachy on the topic of valuing appearance and perceived pedigree over personality or character, it also keeps a light touch, thanks to the Ball (girl) and Top (boy) being non humans.

Although not a classic like "The Steadfast Tin Soldier" or "The Ugly Duckling," "The Loving Pair" provides a glimpse at Andersen's writing in stripped-down form. No lengthy descriptions of life under the sea or in the barnyard happen here. Two of the most basic of nursery toys take center stage, allowing readers to see Andersen using just a few rhetorical flourishes to great effect.

Consider:

- Andersen makes his protagonists as mundane as possible. What could be more everyday than a ball or a top? He could have just as easily made the story about a broom and a bucket. By making the objects laughably ordinary, does Andersen effectively communicate that all people can fall prey to social insecurity and unwise love? Or has Andersen strayed too far into whimsicality with these characters?

- Andersen was unlucky in love in his own life. Indeed, like "The Little Mermaid" and Top, he tended to fall romantically in love with people who were never going to love him back. The most famous case is that of Jenny Lind, a soprano called "The Swedish Nightingale," who did not return his feelings. He proposed marriage; Lind nicely declined. Although Top does not seem to be aiming too high by courting Ball, it's clear after his first declaration that things will not go his way. He seems to accept the rejection reasonably well, but his feelings linger. If you connect this tale with some more famous stories by Andersen, like "The Nightingale" and "The Steadfast Tin Soldier," what messages about love do they contain? How much of Andersen do you see in these stories, if you compare his life with them? (Note: it's not often a good idea to look for much of a writer in his or her works. All writing exists on its own, apart from the author. But Andersen was unusually willing to discuss his identification with his characters who were unlucky in love.)

- Bouncing up to a higher place happens literally and metaphorically in this story. Like Andersen himself, both Ball and Top move up in life (or seem to, in Ball's case). All it takes is a coat of gold paint and a big leap. Is Andersen suggesting that appearances are too important? If so, that's hardly an earth-shattering message. Yet what makes this story intriguing as to social class is that Andersen sees an obsession with appearance in every class. Ball and Top are hardly the crème de la crème of the toy world. (Hhmmm. What would be the top of the social heap in the toy box pecking order?) That everyone is susceptible to class snobbery makes the story a bit trickier. No class is lionized here.

- Ball goes up into the gutter, then back down to a dustbin. Top goes back to the nursery. Not only does Ball end up in the gutter, it's clear that she's irretrievably ruined by her sojourn in the muck. The last paragraph may be the most adult-directed passage in the story. Andersen, who is infamous for the terrible torture his female protagonists undergo, may be using Ball's slip into dirt as a metaphor for women who were "ruined" somehow by men. Does this idea stack up with other terrible fates for the women of Andersen's stories? Or is Ball just a dirty old ball?

- Front story? Back story? Side story? What about that swallow? Does Top ever find a new love in the toy box? Does Ball get repurposed yet again? Does she return to seek revenge on Top?

THE LOVING PAIR

(By Hans Christian Andersen, from *Hans Andersen's Fairy Tales*, edited by J.H. Stickney, 1916)

A whipping Top and a Ball lay close together in a drawer among other playthings. One day the Top said to the Ball, "Since we are living so much together, why should we not be lovers?"

But the Ball, being made of morocco leather, thought herself a very high-bred lady, and would hear nothing of such a proposal.[1] On the next day the little boy to whom the playthings belonged came to the drawer; he painted the Top red and yellow, and drove a bright brass nail right through the head of it; it looked very smart indeed as it spun around after that.

"Look at me," said he to the Ball. "What do you say to me now; why should we not make a match of it, and become man and wife? We suit each other so well! You can jump and I can dance. There would not be a happier pair in the whole world!"

"Do you think so?" said the Ball. "Perhaps you do not know that my father and mother were morocco slippers, and that I have a Spanish cork in my body!"[2]

1) Morocco or Moroccan leather is traditionally red. The Ball (girl's) boast indicates her inflated sense of self worth. A whipping top is one that is whipped into spinning.

2) The whipping Top, a rather humble fellow, foolishly believes that his new look will erase the differences between himself and the ball. Much like people who assume new clothes and new manners in the hope of being accepted into "better" society, only to find their parentage is still held against them, the Top still isn't good enough for a ball with such highly placed "ancestors." As for Spanish cork, it seems that Spain and Portugal are where cork comes from. (I learned this, amazingly enough, at a site about English Cork Cutters.) The reference suggests her exotic and important heritage. Yet she is a bit of a hand-me-down herself, having been repurposed from

(cont.) slippers. Nothing
that the Ball reports
about herself seems
important or
distinguishing, except to
her. Andersen may be
saying that hanging onto
one's roots is silly and
pretentious.

3) *Top gives as good as he*
gets on his noble lineage.
Mahogany is a usually a
high-quality wood and
can be expensive.

4) *Ball is literally and*
figuratively shooting for
something higher. In
Andersen's stories,
yearning literally and
figuratively for a better
world above is an easily
recognized motif. Ball
doesn't seem to recognize
that a free, soaring
swallow is unlikely to be
interested in a child's toy.
In this story, both
characters love
inappropriately. The Ball
is like the title character
in "The Steadfast Tin
Soldier," one of
Andersen's most famous
stories.

"Yes, but then I am made of mahogany," said the Top; "the Mayor himself turned me. He has a turning lathe of his own, and he took great pleasure in making me."[3]

"Can I trust you in this?" asked the Ball.

"May I never be whipped again, if what I tell you is not true," returned the Top.

"You plead your cause well," said the Ball; "but I am not free to listen to your proposal. I am as good as engaged to a swallow. As often as I fly up into the air, he puts his head out of his nest, and says, 'Will you?' In my heart I have said yes to him, and that is almost the same as an engagement; but I'll promise never to forget you."[4]

"A deal of good that will do me," said the Top, and they left off speaking to each other.

Next day the Ball was taken out. The Top saw it fly like a bird into the air—so high that it passed quite out of sight. It came back again; but each time that it touched the earth, it sprang higher than before. This must have been either from its longing to mount higher, like the swallow, or because it had the Spanish cork in its body. On the ninth time the little Ball did not return. The boy sought and sought, but all in vain, for it was gone.[5]

"I know very well where she is," sighed the Top. "She is in the swallow's nest, celebrating her wedding."[6]

The more the Top thought of this the more lovely the Ball became to him; that she could not be his bride seemed to make his love for her the greater. She had preferred another rather than him, but he could not forget her. He twirled round and round, spinning and humming, but always thinking of the Ball, who grew more and more beautiful the more he thought of her. And thus several years passed—it came to be an old love—and now the Top was no longer young!

One day he was gilded all over; never in his life had he been half so handsome. He was now a golden top, and bravely he spun, humming all the time. But once he sprang too high—and was gone![7]

They looked everywhere for him—even in the cellar—but he was nowhere to be found. Where was he?

He had jumped into the dustbin, and lay among cabbage stalks, sweepings, dust, and all sorts of rubbish that had fallen from the gutter in the roof.

"Alas! My gay gilding will soon be spoiled here. What sort of trumpery can I have got among?"[8] And then he peeped at a long cabbage stalk which lay much too near

5) *Three times three—nine times, Ball bounces up and then returns to Earth, soaring, then falling.*

6) *Top easily and readily conceives a simple explanation, which is based on what Ball told him. Not particularly fancy or splendid, he represents an everyman who accepts what others tell him.*

7) *Fancied up, the Top is, at least on the surface, ready to join those above him.*

8) *"Trumpery" is something that is gaudy and fancy, but also of no value. Think of cheap, easily tarnished jewelry.*

9) *The years have not been kind to Ball. She has been sitting in the gutter with garbage, which would suggest she has had time to reflect. Eventually landing in the dustbin doesn't change her either.*

10) *The Top escapes life in the dustbin. He is restored to his rightful place—gilding, we have to assume, intact.*

him, and at something strange and round, which appeared like an apple, but was not. It was an old Ball that must have lain for years in the gutter, and been soaked through and through with water.

"Thank goodness! At last I see an equal; one of my own sort, with whom I can talk," said the Ball, looking earnestly at the gilded Top. "I am myself made of real morocco, sewed together by a young lady's hands, and within my body is a Spanish cork; though no one would think it now. I was very near marrying the swallow, when by a sad chance I fell into the gutter on the roof. I have lain there five years, and I am now wet through and through. You may think what a wearisome situation it has been for a young lady like me."[9]

The Top made no reply. The more he thought of his old love, and the more he heard, the surer he became that this was indeed she.

Then came the housemaid to empty the dustbin. "Hullo!" she cried; "why, here's the gilt Top." And so the Top was brought again to the playroom, to be used and honored as before, while nothing was again heard of the Ball.[10]

And the Top never spoke again of his old love—the feeling must have passed away. And it is not strange, when the object of it has lain five years in a gutter, and been drenched through and through, and when one meets her again in a dustbin.[11]

11) Only one of two central characters has anything like a happy ending to this story. The other is irrevocably ruined by years in the garbage. She has been in the gutter world for too long to be restored to the safety and comfort of a child's nursery. She stays in the dustbin.

THE DIRTY SHEPHERDESS

Introduction

For all that fairy tales focus on coming of age journeys, bad (or foolish) parenting is essential to much of the action in the same stories. Parents abandon their children during famine, and fathers seek to marry their daughters. Mothers (who are not always steps in many versions of classic fairy tales) are jealous of their blossoming daughters. Royal mothers and fathers fail to invite powerful elderly fairies to christenings.

That fairy tales seek to cement parental authority is true. After all, why else would Hansel and Gretel eventually return to the father who colluded in their abandonment? Why would Donkeyskin forgive her father's incestuous machinations? Yet fairy tales also provide endless warnings about bad parenting. "The Dirty Shepherdess" illustrates this well.

While parents and children often play the "I love you this much" game, it has its perils. Parents may not always get the answer they crave. Or, the child may answer insincerely. "The Dirty Shepherdess" puts me in mind of the movie, *The Bad Seed* (1956), in which the smarmy Rhoda Penmark, a delightfully evil girl, engages in the following routine with her father:

Rhoda: "What will you give me for a basket of kisses?"

Dad: "A basket of kisses? Why, I'll give you a basket of hugs."†

Rhoda's frequently absent father is easily taken in by Rhoda, because, like all parents, he wants to believe his child adores him. But the silliness of the question is used to illustrate how manipulative Rhoda is. That he is asking the question is part of the problem of Rhoda's evil. The warning in the movie and in fairy tales: parents shouldn't ask about a child's love unless they are willing to hear the truth or are accepting of lies.

Returning to "The Dirty Shepherdess," consider that while the apple is known as a humble fruit, it is a humble, *pretty* fruit. It's far more glamorous than poor old salt. Yet humans can live without apples, but we cannot live without salt (sodium). The heroine of our story is telling her father that her love is an essential element, but he is too foolish to recognize this.

"Love like salt" fairy tales exist across Western Europe and in India. I picked this version in part because I love the title. How can anyone read this title and not wonder what in the world it is about? But that the tension in the story is caused by an unwise question from a parent seeking reassurance is what makes the story resonate. Fairy tales are deeply concerned with sin, and the king in this tale is both proud and vain. His question is the original sin of the story.

Consider:
- Shakespeare's *King Lear* immediately springs to mind when considering "The Dirty Shepherdess." In both narratives, Cordelia and the shepherdess give short answers to the king's questions about love, while Regan and Goneril, Cordelia's sisters, give detailed, fawning replies. Even when Lear reminds Cordelia that her royal inheritance is at stake, she declines to be insincere. Does the shepherdess's elder sister seem false like Regan and Goneril? Why? If so, can the elder sister be blamed for wanting her father's approval as well as a kingdom? After all, a kingdom is at stake. ‡

- The shepherdess is unwilling to compromise about giving her father an honest answer about her love, showing real strength of character, yet when she is banished from the kingdom, she meekly follows orders. Why? The most obvious answer is that she's the heroine of a fairy tale and fairy tales tend to reinforce parental authority, but as is often the case, dueling moral messages play out in this story. On the one hand, she is supposed to be true to herself and honest about her love for her father. On the other, she then does what she is told, at great cost to herself. Which value is treated as more important in the story?

- We get very little information about the ways in which the heroine is pretty. How might she be described physically? While "Snow White," for example, details how the heroine looks, in this story, we only know the princess is pretty. Does the vagueness about her looks help make her easy to identify with? She can be of any race or country, any size or shape, aged 16 or 25. How does she look in your mind? Does it matter? Another area to explore: Does the lack of specificity about beauty type make it more or less of an endorsement about rigid expectations of female beauty?

- The Dirty Shepherdess is no fool. She doesn't seem to have many options at this point for regaining her place as a royal. The story is ambiguous about whether or not she intentionally puts the ring in the bread dough, but it seems probable that she did, given the effort she put into the task. Does it matter if she does? Is she too devious if she plants the ring?

- The story ends with a celebration of tasty food. More than any other story in this book, this story highlights the importance of food in fairy tales. Compare this tale to "Hansel and Gretel," in which the lack of food is the main focus, as opposed to unsalted, tasteless food. In what way do the stories complicate or reinforce each other about food? For example, in "Hansel and Gretel," wanting to eat the house is not solely linked to their starvation. Hansel assures Gretel the house will be delicious and strongly encourages her to eat the window. No one starves in "The Dirty Shepherdess," but that doesn't mean the story doesn't reflect the concerns of poor people, as stories like "Hansel and Gretel" do.

Or, imagine describing the delicious dishes the king enjoys at the end of the story. What would be on the menu? What about salads, sauces and sweets? Salt is part of most dishes.

Source Notes

† "Memorable Quotes for The Bad Seed." *IMDb*. Accessed August 27, 2012.

‡ "To Love My Father All." D.L. Ashliman's Home Page. Accessed August 27, 2012.

THE DIRTY SHEPHERDESS

(From *The Green Fairy Book*, by Andrew Lang, 1892)

Once upon a time there lived a king who had two daughters, and he loved them with all his heart. When they grew up, he was suddenly seized with a wish to know if they, on their part, truly loved him, and he made up his mind that he would give his kingdom to whichever best proved her devotion.[1]

So he called the elder princess and said to her, "How much do you love me?"

"As the apple of my eye!" answered she.[2]

"Ah!" exclaimed the king, kissing her tenderly as he spoke, "you are indeed a good daughter."

Then he sent for the younger, and asked her how much she loved him.

"I look upon you, my father," she answered, "as I look upon salt in my food."[3]

But the king did not like her words, and ordered her to quit the court, and never again to appear before him. The poor princess went sadly up to her

1) *Are the demands by aging kings in fairy tales, plays, and myths meant to signify a cognitive slip? These fairy tales of parental demands and child exile seem like games of heartache and political expediency. After all, an extra heir sloping around is apt to lead to factions.*

2) *Big sister goes for the cliché. The apple is always safe. Or is it? We need only look to the Garden of Eden to see the kind of trouble apples can cause, and early listeners of this story would have known the story of the fall all too well. The tale of "Snow White" also warns us of the perils of the alluring apple.*

3) *The younger daughter's answer hints at a pleasing simplicity and practicality. While the apple is certainly a useful fruit, salt is essential to life. It preserves food, flavors it, can be used to clean, to melt ice. Yet it can sting and*

(cont.) burn as well.

4) *Our heroine may not be adept at all the housewifely arts, but here, she is exercising the same practical good sense she demonstrated when she compared her love of her father to her love of salt. Most sensible housewives would not want an extremely pretty girl in their homes. They have daughters to marry off, sons to keep out of trouble, male servants to keep in line—not to mention husbands. The reverse, of course, is also true. For example, handsome footmen were considered desirable in noble households, because they looked good in livery, but they were also considered a potential source of domestic disruption. Fairy tales, however, tend to concern themselves with what women think and feel, even as they uphold male dominance.*

5) *Then again, no one wants a pig at the dinner table, unless it has an apple stuffed in its mouth and is about to be carved. The protagonist has disguised herself a touch too well.*

room and began to cry, but when she was reminded of her father's commands, she dried her eyes, and made a bundle of her jewels and her best dresses and hurriedly left the castle where she was born.

She walked straight along the road in front of her, without knowing very well where she was going or what was to become of her, for she had never been shown how to work, and all she had learnt consisted of a few household rules, and receipts of dishes which her mother had taught her long ago. And as she was afraid that no housewife would want to engage a girl with such a pretty face, she determined to make herself as ugly as she could.[4]

She therefore took off the dress that she was wearing and put on some horrible old rags belonging to a beggar, all torn and covered with mud. After that she smeared mud all over her hands and face, and shook her hair into a great tangle. Having thus changed her appearance, she went about offering herself as a goose-girl or shepherdess. But the farmers' wives would have nothing to say to such a dirty maiden, and sent her away with a morsel of bread for charity's sake.[5]

After walking for a great many days

without being able to find any work, she came to a large farm where they were in want of a shepherdess, and engaged her gladly.[6]

One day when she was keeping her sheep in a lonely tract of land, she suddenly felt a wish to dress herself in her robes of splendor. She washed herself carefully in the stream, and as she always carried her bundle with her, it was easy to shake off her rags, and transform herself in a few moments into a great lady.[7]

The king's son, who had lost his way out hunting, perceived this lovely damsel a long way off, and wished to look at her closer. But as soon as the girl saw what he was at, she fled into the wood as swiftly as a bird. The prince ran after her, but as he was running he caught his foot in the root of a tree and fell, and when he got up again, she was nowhere to be seen.[8]

When she was quite safe, she put on her rags again, and smeared over her face and hands. However the young prince, who was both hot and thirsty, found his way to the farm, to ask for a drink of cider, and he inquired the name of the beautiful lady that kept the sheep. At this everyone began to laugh, for they said

6) *The dirty shepherdess has succeeded completely with her disguise. Unrecognizable, cast out from even simple farm families, she is enduring the period of loneliness that occurs so often in myths and folklore, as part of her hero's journey. Like Andersen's little mermaid, who must give up her voice to gain a chance at romantic love and an immortal soul, the shepherdess must endure a painful transformation as part of her story.*

7) *Unlike other fairy tale heroines, who have talking dolls or a fairy godmother, the shepherdess has only her own good sense and a nice dress to ease her travails. But clearly she has learned one of the golden rules of fashion: have at least one really good outfit.*

8) *Who needs Prince Charming when we have The Peeping Prince? Consider Snow White, in her crystal coffin. In many versions, the prince is so smitten at the mere sight of her, he offers to buy her. Snow is unconscious, of course. Indeed, the prince believes she is dead. Then there is Sleeping Beauty. Being gawked at and*

(cont.) smooched is the least of her woes. Read "Sun, Moon and Talia," in which the unsuspecting sleeping heroine does not wake up until after her twins are born. Yes, twins. Yet the heroine catches on quickly in this story, making the prince a far more sympathetic character than in other, more famous tales.

9) Why is it that in fairy tales, the application of dirt and ugly old clothes is usually a sufficient disguise for stunningly beautiful women? Can mere dirt obliterate perfect teeth, shining eyes, good cheekbones, and the glow of good health? Class differences may explain, in part, why dirt and tattered clothes rendered beauty invisible, but isn't this theme one of the least believable in fairy tales?

10) Princes are seldom truly charming in fairy tales. (See #8.) Yet this fellow is sensitive enough to fear ridicule, but delighted enough by the heroine to pine for her. On the other hand, wasting away for love seems obsessive, which may land him back in the unwholesome, icky prince category.

that the shepherdess was one of the ugliest and dirtiest creatures under the sun.[9]

The prince thought some witchcraft must be at work, and he hastened away before the return of the shepherdess, who became that evening the butt of everybody's jests.

But the king's son thought often of the lovely maiden whom he had only seen for a moment, though she seemed to him much more fascinating than any lady of the court. At last he dreamed of nothing else, and grew thinner day by day till his parents inquired what the matter was, promising to do all they could to make him as happy as he once was. He dared not tell them the truth, lest they should laugh at him, so he only said that he should like some bread baked by the kitchen girl in the distant farm.[10]

Although the wish appeared rather odd, they hastened to fulfill it, and the farmer was told the request of the king's son. The maiden showed no surprise at receiving such an order, but merely asked for some flour, salt, and water, and also that she might be left alone in a little room adjoining the oven, where the kneading-trough stood. Before beginning her work she washed herself carefully, and even put on her rings; but, while she was baking, one of her rings slid into the dough. When she had finished she dirtied herself again, and let lumps of the dough stick to her fingers, so that she became as ugly as before.[11]

The loaf, which was a very little one, was brought to the king's son, who ate it with pleasure. But in cutting it he found the ring of the princess, and declared to his parents that he would marry the girl whom that ring fitted.

So the king made a proclamation through his whole kingdom, and ladies came from afar to lay claim to the honor. But the ring was so tiny that even those who had the smallest hands could only get it on their little fingers. In a short time all the maidens of the kingdom, including the peasant girls, had tried on the ring, and the king was just about to announce that their efforts had been in vain, when the prince observed that he had not yet seen the shepherdess.[12]

They sent to fetch her, and she arrived covered with rags, but with her hands cleaner than usual, so that she could easily slip on the ring. The king's son declared that he would fulfill his promise, and when his parents mildly remarked that the girl was only a keeper of sheep, and a very ugly one too, the maiden boldly said that she was born a princess, and that, if they would only

11) This paragraph provides us with another reason to identify with and like the dirty shepherdess. She is hard to fluster, determined, and practical. No wonder she knows the true value of salt.

12) Like her famous fairy-tale sister, "Cinderella," the dirty shepherdess is essentially finely made, with small hands and feet. Hands were especially important to beauty in the past, as smooth, soft hands suggested a life of leisure. Presumably, the shepherdess had not been working in the fields so long that she ruined her hands.

13) Ever practical, the princess is not about to stand by meekly and forfeit her place by the prince's side. With a little soap and water and that trusty good dress, the dirty shepherdess is no more and the princess is ready for her close-up.

14) Unlike most fairy-tale parents, who are usually absent, foolish, or cruel, the prince's parents seem like rather kindly folks, ready to hear and accept a rather implausible story. At worst, they could be accused of indulging their son overmuch.

15) The fact that the princess's father has begun to see the error of his ways before the wedding suggests that this story will have a true happily ever after for the families involved. His daughter's acceptance of him after his cruel rejection seems more palatable to the reader, as her father began to mend his ways on his own.

give her some water and leave her alone in a room for a few minutes, she would show that she could look as well as anyone in fine clothes.[13]

They did what she asked, and when she entered in a magnificent dress, she looked so beautiful that all saw she must be a princess in disguise. The king's son recognized the charming damsel of whom he had once caught a glimpse, and, flinging himself at her feet, asked if she would marry him. The princess then told her story, and said that it would be necessary to send an ambassador to her father to ask his consent and to invite him to the wedding.[14]

The princess's father, who had never ceased to repent his harshness towards his daughter, had sought her through the land, but as no one could tell him anything of her, he supposed her dead. Therefore it was with great joy he heard that she was living and that a king's son asked her in marriage, and he quitted his kingdom with his elder daughter so as to be present at the ceremony.[15]

By the orders of the bride, they only served her father at the wedding breakfast bread without salt, and meat without seasoning. Seeing him make faces, and eat very little, his daughter, who sat beside him, inquired if his dinner was not to his taste.

"No," he replied, "the dishes are

carefully cooked and sent up, but they are all so dreadfully tasteless."

"Did not I tell you, my father, that salt was the best thing in life? And yet, when I compared you to salt, to show how much I loved you, you thought slightingly of me and you chased me from your presence."

The king embraced his daughter, and allowed that he had been wrong to misinterpret her words. Then, for the rest of the wedding feast they gave him bread made with salt, and dishes with seasoning, and he said they were the very best he had ever eaten.

THE GIFTS OF THE LITTLE PEOPLE

Introduction

Fairies are tricky devils, as this story shows. They take as much as they give, sometimes more than they give, and are easily offended. The beings in this tale could be elves, and as lovers of folklore and fantasy can tell you, elves cannot always be trusted. On the other hand, dwarfs are often described as more benign, as in the story of "Snow White," in which, according to the Brothers' Grimm, the little men are not just kind to Snow, but have a home that is as clean as can be.

The spirits of our story are not officially named, but they are small, like elves and dwarfs. We don't know if the little people are beautiful, as fairies often are, but we do know they play lovely music—music so lovely, it tempts the human traveler. Whatever type of supernatural beings the spirits may be, they will not give something for nothing. They demand subservience from the tailor and the blacksmith, in the form of cutting their beards and shaving their heads. Wisely, the human men don't fight the shaving.

Of the two travelers, it is the tailor who proves sensible in his dealings with the mountain spirits. Greed is often dealt with harshly in fairy tales, and "The Gifts of the Little People," provides a first-rate example. The tailor ends up well off and happy. Probably.

"Probably," takes us to the trouble with gifts from fairies. Despite promises of happily ever after and the supposed goodness of beautiful princesses and the lure of Princes Charming, much of what is good is also a liability in fairy tales. Especially when the good comes from fairies. In "Fairy Gifts," also in this book, the Flower Fairy's gifts cannot stop her charges from making mistakes in the outside world. In "Frau Holle," the "good girl" ends up covered in gold, which seems deeply uncomfortable.

The blacksmith makes the fateful error of going back to the spirits for more gold. The travelers were lucky they escaped with shaving the first time, *and*, the gold they received was not something they truly earned through work. As soon as we read that the blacksmith is returning, we know his fate is sealed. Indeed, the fact that he ends up with the tailor and his family is surprising, given his greed. Were he the "bad girl" in "Frau Holle," he'd be covered in pitch and left without a home.

Consider:
- The tailor is a stock, simple kind of character. He could easily have been a miller or a miller's son or a shoe cobbler. His key trait is that he lacks greed and is humble. Humble folks are often rewarded in fairy tales. Yet, do stories that exalt humble characters reinforce social classes? Do they encourage audiences to stay in their places? Granted, the poor heroes of these stories often end up wealthy, or at least reasonably so, as is the case for the tailor, but they remain simple souls, everymen, at heart. They do not lose the essence of the peasant. Would a message upholding acceptance of the simple life help keep the impoverished content? In other words, just stay in your place and be content, and maybe you can run across spirits who will make you rich. (Note: it's fair to point out that it's not just

poor heroes who are rewarded for modest attitudes. Princes and princesses are as well. Maria Tatar discusses this in *The Hard Facts of Grimms' Fairy Tales*.)

- For all that greed is punished in fairy tales, it can be rewarded as well. The hero of "Jack and the Beanstalk" is a thief, in most versions. Hansel and Gretel are unquestionably victims of famine, but did they actually need to eat the witch out of house and home when they encounter the gingerbread house? (Bettelheim's ideas on oral greed in "Hansel and Gretel" are hard to endorse, but that doesn't make him wrong about everything. See "Hansel and Gretel" in Tatar's *The Classic Fairy Tales*.) The greedy king in "Rumpelstiltskin" retains his wife and his child, even though he is a thoroughly reprehensible character. What to make of the dual message of tales? Does this make fairy tales essentially problematic as a genre? Or does the spectrum of outcome for greed and its lack suggest that fairy tales accurately reflect the complex reality of human behavior?

- When heroes of fairy tales are rewarded with gold, I often wonder, how much good would gold do people from a small town hundreds of years ago? There were no local banks, no ATMs. It seems the acquisition of gold would also seem hard to explain to neighbors and family. Although many people believed in spirits and elves hundreds of years ago, many didn't as well, so the gifts of the little people might be hard to explain away. Might the tailor be accused of stealing? How would he convert the money? More importantly, is it possible the gold is symbolic of improved wealth and status and not meant to be literally interpreted?

- A new layer of fairy lore and dangerous allure is added to each paragraph. The travelers have chanced upon some fairy celebration—perhaps Midsummer's Eve? Or is it possible that the gathering is being held specifically for the purpose of testing the tailor and the blacksmith? Is there a specific lesson that both the main characters and fairy tale audiences are meant to learn from this story? If so, is greed the only focus for moralizing here? What about the benefits of healthy fear, like the tailor has? What about the benefit of romantic love, which appears to be a higher value than wealth in this story?

- The tailor clearly is the hero of this story. But does the tale actually have a happy ending for the tailor? The fact that he is stuck with the poor blacksmith—whose baldness, it seems, may be a big deal—suggests that the tailor has been too generous. What does the future seem like for the tailor and his family (if he has one)? What would their after story read like? Isn't it likely that the blacksmith might do something boneheaded again? Would the tailor be free of the little people or find himself lured there again?

THE GIFTS OF THE LITTLE PEOPLE

(From *Grimm's Fairy Tales*, edited by
Edna Henry Lee Turpin, 1903)

A blacksmith and a tailor had been at work all day. In the evening they walked together in the country. The moon rose as they were on a lonely road.[1]

All at once they heard far-off music. It was so sweet that they forgot how tired they were and hurried forward. The sound grew clearer and clearer. Soon they came to a hillside. There they saw a crowd of merry little men and women. They were dancing in a ring to the sound of music.[2] In the middle of the ring was a little man with a long white beard which reached to his waist. He wore a coat of many colors.[3]

The tailor and the blacksmith stood still watching the dancers. Soon the little old man made signs for them to come inside the ring. At first they did not wish to do this. But when they saw how merry and good-natured the little people were, they entered the ring. Round and round danced the little men and women.

1) *The difference between the two main characters in this story is apparent from the beginning. Tailors were not traditionally the richest craftsmen, although they could make a good living. It's safe to assume that a blacksmith would be wealthier and more powerful in the village than a tailor. That the two travelers will have wildly different fates is foreshadowed by their professions.*

2) *A new layer of fairy lore and dangerous allure is added to each paragraph. The travelers have chanced upon some fairy celebration—perhaps Midsummer's Eve? Or is it possible that the gathering is being held specifically for the purpose of testing the tailor and the blacksmith?*

3) *The long, white beard is also a sign of the head man's wisdom and power. He is*

(cont.) central to the
gathering both literally
and figuratively. His "coat
of many colors" is a direct
reference to Joseph, from
the Old Testament, who
wore such a coat as his
father's favorite child.

4) While shaving one's head
and beard are common
practices among men
nowadays, beards
especially denoted the
status of manhood in
times past. By shaving
the tailor and the
goldsmith, the
conspicuously bearded
head fairy is asserting his
dominance. In a sense,
the travelers have been
vanquished. It's like
castration through
barbering.

5) It's midnight, the
traditional witching
hour, and even the fairies
are leaving, so it's
definitely time for the
tailor and the blacksmith
to hit the road.

After a while the old man drew a large knife from his belt. He felt the edge and sharpened it on a stone. Then he turned and looked hard at the strangers. They were frightened, but they had no time to run away. He caught the blacksmith and shaved off his hair and beard. Then he turned to the tailor and shaved him too.[4]

After doing this he patted them on their backs to show that he was pleased with them. He pointed to a heap of coals on the roadside, and made signs to them to fill their pockets.

Both obeyed, though they could not see what would be the use of a pocket full of coals.

Now the clock struck twelve. All at once the music stopped and in a flash the little people were gone. There lay the green hillside in the moonlight.[5]

The tailor and the blacksmith rubbed their eyes. Was it all a dream? No. There were their shaven heads and there were their pockets full of coals.

They walked down the road till they came to a house where they wished to spend the night. There was nowhere for them to sleep but in the stable. They lay down on the straw and fell asleep. They were too tired even to take the coals out of their pockets.

But early the next morning the weight awakened them. What was their surprise to find that instead of coals their pockets were full of lumps of gold. Their beards, too, had grown again and their heads were covered with hair.[6]

They were now very rich. The blacksmith had larger pockets and he had even more gold than the tailor. But he was not content.

"Ah, friend tailor," he said, "I wish we had known those coals would change to gold, I should have taken more, I should have filled my hands as well as my pockets. Let us go back to the hillside tonight. No doubt the little old man will give us more."[7]

"No" said the tailor. "I am content. The little man gave me more gold than I had ever hoped to see. Instead of trying to get more, I will make the best of what I have."

"Then I will go alone," said the blacksmith. He had the tailor make his pockets larger, and he bought two great bags. Then he went to the hillside. He found the little people dancing and singing as on the former night.

Again they took him into the ring. The old man shaved him and made signs to him to take some coals.[8] He filled all his pockets and both the bags. Then he went home dragging his heavy load. He had a bed that night, but he did not take

6) *A brand new day and a fresh start for the tailor and the blacksmith. They have hair! They have beards! They have gold! Yet, despite all the excitement of their visit with the fairies, and the freshly-discovered riches, the true test of character begins now.*

7) *There is often one threatening sin in fairy tales, and the blacksmith is almost a personification of greed. Like Jack, who can't resist running up the beanstalk again, after he gets the goose who lays the golden eggs, the blacksmith is going give the fairies another run. What are the chances this will end well for him? He seems like the kind of diner who will keep going back for more food at an all-you-can-eat buffet just because he wants to take advantage, not because he enjoys the food.*

8) *The contrast between the tailor and the blacksmith now has perfect clarity. The blacksmith boldly goes back to the fairies, who seem to allow him to take what he wants— for the price of symbolically unmanning him again.*

off his clothes.

"The weight of the gold in my pockets will wake me early," he said. "Then I will rise and count my riches."

Early the next morning he started up and put his hands in his pockets. There were coals, black coals. Handful after handful he pulled out, but no gold. In the bags, too, there were only coals.

"Well, I still have the gold I got the first night," he said. "That is safe." And he went to look at it.

Alas! It was all turned to coal. He put his smutty hands up to his head. It was bald and his chin was smooth.[9]

"Alas," he cried. "I am punished for being greedy. I wanted more, and I have lost what I had." And he began to groan so loud that he woke the tailor.[10]

"Do not be so sad," said the tailor. "You and I have long been friends. I have more gold than I need and you shall share it."

He kept his word, but he could not put back the blacksmith's hair. As long as he lived he had to wear a cap to hide his bald head.[11]

9) *"Beware of fairies bearing gifts," is one of the primary warnings of fairy lore. Fairies are capricious and easily annoyed. "Going back to the well," so to speak, is almost always a bad idea. See "The Fisherman and His Wife" for an extreme example.*

10) *Bald, beardless, and broke, the blacksmith has been effectively punished for his sins. In a time when men wore beards regularly, and head shaving was not at all in fashion, his lack of hair would have made him notable in the village.*

11) *The tailor seems almost too good to be true at this point. Generous and kind, he also may be a bit clueless about what his future with the blacksmith will actually be like.*

THE BLUE LIGHT

Introduction

Fairy tales are frequently sources for social commentary. Kings and queens are as foolish about children as peasants are. Animals like "Puss in Boots" can make noblemen of a simple miller's son through the artful application of well-chosen gifts, scamming for some fine clothes, and some strategic appropriation of estates. A naked emperor believes he wears a splendid outfit.

This story starts out making no bones about how badly soldiers were treated during and after wars. That rulers can be utterly indifferent to the plight of the men who actually fought in wars is clear by the end of the third sentence. Fairy tales may be bursting with criticism about rulers, but this story is unusually blatant about how the powerful break contracts with poor workers.

By the end of this tale, the soldier seems as cruel as the king. He violates the princess by forcing her to perform chores while asleep. Even the usual fairy tale assertion about love—that a prince or hero in the story sees a princess and is immediately struck by her beauty, doesn't happen here. No mention is made of her character, either.

The soldier himself is not young or old. He is wounded and sad at the beginning of "The Blue Light." He does have a simple, guileless quality found often in fairy tale heroes. He accepts help when offered, even if he is bewildered, and isn't especially curious.

Things happen. He's not sure why. A lack of curiosity about "why" is a male characteristic in fairy tales. Women who cannot avoid curiosity are brought to doom or near doom. "Sleeping Beauty" cannot help finding the spindle, because she cannot help exploring the castle. "Snow White" cannot help herself—she has to open the door to the peddler woman. Yet Jack in "Jack and the Beanstalk" is remarkably uncurious about where his magic beans actually come from—even though he does climb up the beanstalk very eagerly. The miller's son in "Puss and Boots" seems not at all interested in how his cat came to walk, talk, and plot.

As social commentary, the message in "The Blue Light" seems to be that everyone, given the opportunity, will behave selfishly or stupidly. The simple earnestness of the common folk is not celebrated here. The divine right of kings is not upheld. The witch loses her chance at treasure because she can't control her temper.

If there is a "good character" here, it may be the black dwarf. "The Blue Light" obviously has shades of "Aladdin and the Magic Lamp" in it, with a "bound" supernatural character in the form of the dwarf. Despite being compelled to help the soldier, rather than voluntarily doing so, the dwarf tries to counsel the increasingly vengeful soldier about his actions.

Many fairy tales do not end with happily ever after, but most are a bit more uplifting than this one. If there is a moral message here, it's that power corrupts all humans.

Consider:
- Colors are important in this story. The light is blue. The dwarf is black. In many fairy tales, color is clearly stated and seems significant. Think of "Snow White," "The Red Shoes," "Little Red Riding Hood." Gold shines and silver gleams. Beanstalks seem brilliantly green. Audiences want color, and lots of it, in fairy tales. Using "The Blue Light"

and one or two other tales as examples, how does the use of color seem to heighten the appeal of fairy tales? Why?

- The witch never appears again in this story after leaving the soldier in a huff. Why not? Does this seem like an oversight on the part of the storytellers? Why does she vanish so completely? After all, she gets the story action rolling pretty thoroughly. What does her disappearance say about attitudes toward poor old women in fairy tales? Does it have to say anything?

- While the significance of female characters (and the problematic nature of them) is pretty well examined in fairy tale scholarship and popular culture, the princess in this story is unusually insubstantial. If you could write a story for the princess, what would it be? *Who* would she be? Would she have an after story? Would she love the soldier? Would he love her? Revenge is the lifeblood of this story, and if anyone deserves to get some, it's the princess. How would she give back what she got? If you wouldn't write her a story, why not?

- The transformation of the soldier from a regular guy into a payback machine worthy of a Hollywood movie franchise is startling. It's also subversive, because not only is the king pegged as a bad ruler from early on in the story (not uncommon in folklore), but the soldier does not seem potentially any better. No positive social order is suggested at the end of the story. There is no attempt to soften him once he is bent on his harsh course. There's no love. There's no moral message to impart. Does this help explain why the tale is less popular than "The Tinder Box," for instance? Or

"Aladdin" stories? In the latter two, neither man is a perfect person, but at least they are shown to feel tenderness toward the princesses they marry.

- Imagine the kingdom after the soldier takes control. What would happen? Why? Are there any clues about him in the original that would suggest he could be a fit ruler? Or would he eventually lose everything and end up where he began?

THE BLUE LIGHT

(From *Fairy Tales By The Brothers Grimm*, by
Edgar Taylor and Marian Edwardes, 1876)

There was once upon a time a soldier who for many years had served the king faithfully, but when the war came to an end, could serve no longer because of the many wounds which he had received.

The king said to him: "You may return to your home, I need you no longer, and you will not receive any more money, for he only receives wages who renders me service for them."[1]

Then the soldier did not know how to earn a living, went away greatly troubled, and walked the whole day, until in the evening he entered a forest. When darkness came on, he saw a light, which he went up to, and came to a house wherein lived a witch.

"Do give me one night's lodging, and a little to eat and drink," said he to her, "or I shall starve."

"Oho!" she answered, "who gives anything to a run-away soldier? Yet will I be compassionate, and take you in, if you will do what I wish."[2]

"What do you wish?" said the soldier.

1) *Soldiers the world over were historically treated badly once they were injured or wars had ended. Lauded while useful, they often were badly paid (or not paid at all). Already passionate about German folklore and history, the Brothers Grimm were intensely affected by Napoleon's victory in what is now Germany. It seems the subject of war was fraught for them.*

2) *Sympathy for the plight of soldiers only went so far, and the witch's disdain for the protagonist demonstrates that it wasn't only royalty and nobility who disdained soldiers. Common folk did as well.*

3) *Food is at the heart of many a fairy tale, and often comes at a great price. Already in poor physical shape, the soldier is forced into more backbreaking labor, making the witch entirely unsympathetic.*

4) *The witch doesn't get what she wants because she won't negotiate. Anger is expensive. Despite her own investment in exploiting the soldier's labor, she stomps away, investing no more cunning or negotiation into the transaction with the soldier.*

"That you should dig all round my garden for me, tomorrow." The soldier consented, and next day labored with all his strength, but could not finish it by the evening.

"I see well enough," said the witch, "that you can do no more today, but I will keep you yet another night, in payment for which you must tomorrow chop me a load of wood, and chop it small."

The soldier spent the whole day in doing it, and in the evening the witch proposed that he should stay one night more. "Tomorrow, you shall only do me a very trifling piece of work. Behind my house, there is an old dry well, into which my light has fallen, it burns blue, and never goes out, and you shall bring it up again."[3]

Next day the old woman took him to the well, and let him down in a basket. He found the blue light, and made her a signal to draw him up again. She did draw him up, but when he came near the edge, she stretched down her hand and wanted to take the blue light away from him.

"No," said he, perceiving her evil intention, "I will not give you the light until I am standing with both feet upon the ground." The witch fell into a passion, let him fall again into the well, and went away.[4]

The poor soldier fell without injury on the moist ground, and the blue light went on burning, but of what use was that to him? He saw very well that he could not escape death. He sat for a while very sorrowfully, then suddenly he felt in his pocket and found his tobacco pipe, which was still half full. "This shall be my last pleasure," thought he, pulled it out, lit it at the blue light and began to smoke.[5]

When the smoke had circled about the cavern, suddenly a little black dwarf stood before him, and said, "Lord, what are your commands?"[6]

"What my commands are?" replied the soldier, quite astonished.

"I must do everything you bid me," said the little man.

"Good," said the soldier; "then in the first place help me out of this well." The little man took him by the hand, and led him through an underground passage, but he did not forget to take the blue light with him. On the way the dwarf showed him the treasures which the witch had collected and hidden there, and the soldier took as much gold as he could carry.

When he was above, he said to the little man: "Now go and bind the old witch, and carry her before the judge."[7]

In a short time she came by like the wind, riding on a wild tom-cat and screaming frightfully.[8]

5) The soldier is unhappily resigned to his fate, but has faced death before. While it is still early in the story, he has thus far demonstrated endurance, a bit of craftiness, and patient resignation.

6) The color of the dwarf may just be a detail to make the story more interesting, or it may be some connection to the Black Forest in Germany.

7) Laid back and simple by nature though he may be, the soldier demonstrates that the downtrodden will seek revenge if given the opportunity. In addition, just because he's uncomplicated, doesn't mean the soldier is stupid. Inspired by a need for payback, he guides the action of the rest of story. Unlike crafty helpers (like Puss in Boots) the dwarf really is a slave to the desires of his master; he is not a strategist or a general. In this case, the dwarf is the foot soldier. How quickly roles have changed for the soldier.

8) *The cat may signify a witch's familiar.*

9) *The soldier now wants revenge, an emotion closely linked to wrath, which is a sin and often punished in fairy tales like "Rumpelstiltskin," and "Snow White." Revenge belongs to God, according to the Bible. Yet the hero of this story will use the dwarf to wreak terrible revenge.*

10) *The dwarf may be forced to do the soldier's bidding, but his question suggests an attachment is forming between himself and the soldier—at least on the side of the dwarf. He will question the soldier again, but the soldier becomes increasingly arrogant in his decision making.*

Nor was it long before the little man reappeared. "It is all done," said he, "and the witch is already hanging on the gallows. What further commands has my lord?" inquired the dwarf.

"At this moment, none," answered the soldier. "You can return home, only be at hand immediately, if I summon you."

"Nothing more is needed than that you should light your pipe at the blue light, and I will appear before you at once." Thereupon he vanished from his sight.

The soldier returned to the town from which he came. He went to the best inn, ordered himself handsome clothes, and then bade the landlord furnish him a room as handsome as possible. When it was ready and the soldier had taken possession of it, he summoned the little black manikin and said, "I have served the king faithfully, but he has dismissed me, and left me to hunger, and now I want to take my revenge."[9]

"What am I to do?" asked the little man.

"Late at night, when the king's daughter is in bed, bring her here in her sleep, she shall do servant's work for me."

The dwarf said: "That is an easy thing for me to do, but a very dangerous thing for you, for if it is discovered, you will fare ill."[10]

When twelve o'clock had struck, the door sprang open, and the little man carried in the princess. "Aha! are you there?" cried the soldier, "get to your work at once! Fetch the broom and sweep the chamber." When she had done this, he ordered her to come to his chair, and then he stretched out his feet and said, "Pull off my boots," and then he threw them in her face, and made her pick them up again, and clean and brighten them. She, however, did everything he bade her, without opposition, silently and with half-shut eyes. When the first cock crowed, the dwarf carried her back to the royal palace, and laid her in her bed.[11]

Next morning when the princess arose she went to her father, and told him that she had had a very strange dream. "I was carried through the streets with the rapidity of lightning," said she, "and taken into a soldier's room, and I had to wait upon him like a servant, sweep his room, clean his boots, and do all kinds of menial work. It was only a dream, and yet I am just as tired as if I really had done everything."

"The dream may have been true," said the king. "I will give you a piece of advice. Fill your pocket full of peas, and make a small hole in the pocket, and then if you are carried away again, they will fall out and leave a track in the streets."[12] But unseen by the king, the dwarf was standing beside him when he said that, and heard all. At night when the sleeping princess was again carried through the streets, some peas certainly did

11) That the soldier is using a sort of mind control over the king's daughter moves him one step closer to being the sort of man the king seems to be at the beginning of the story: exploitative. Forcing the princess to do backbreaking work while she has no power at all smacks of the same kind of ruthlessness of which her father is guilty.

12) Once again, echoes of another fairy tale show up in "The Blue Light." This time, "Hansel and Gretel." Also, the entire story has an "Aladdin" feel to it, not to mention, Andersen's "The Tinder Box."

13) The king can't ultimately vanquish the soldier, because the soldier has supernatural* help.

14) The dwarf's alleged inability to stop the king's "shoe plan" is hard to believe. Why not just make a lot of shoes? After all, the dwarf does have magical powers. Or, does the princess's shoe, as a personal object of hers, have its own symbolic magic that a dwarf cannot overcome? A third option: Is the dwarf simply trying to save the soldier from his desire for revenge?

fall out of her pocket, but they made no track, for the crafty little man had just before scattered peas in every street there was. And again the princess was compelled to do servant's work until cock-crow.

Next morning the king sent his people out to seek the track, but it was all in vain, for in every street poor children were sitting, picking up peas, and saying, "It must have rained peas, last night."[13]

"We must think of something else," said the king. "Keep your shoes on when you go to bed, and before you come back from the place where you are taken, hide one of them there, I will soon contrive to find it."

The dwarf heard this plot, and at night when the soldier again ordered him to bring the princess, revealed it to him, and told him that he knew of no expedient to counteract this stratagem, and that if the shoe were found in the soldier's house it would go badly with him.[14] "Do what I bid you," replied the soldier, and again this third night the princess was obliged to work like a servant, but before she went away, she hid her shoe under the bed.

Next morning the king had the entire town searched for his daughter's shoe. It was found at the soldier's, and the soldier himself, who at the entreaty of the dwarf had gone outside the gate, was soon brought back, and thrown into prison. In his flight he had forgotten the most valuable things he had, the blue light and the gold, and had only one ducat in his pocket. And now loaded with chains, he was standing at the window of his dungeon, when he chanced to see one of his comrades passing by.

The soldier tapped at the pane of glass, and when this man came up, said to him, "Be so kind as to fetch me the small bundle I have left lying in the inn, and I will give you a ducat for doing it." His comrade ran thither and brought him what he wanted. As soon as the soldier was alone again, he lighted his pipe and summoned the dwarf.

"Have no fear," said the latter to his master. "Go wheresoever they take you, and let them do what they will, only take the blue light with you."[15] Next day the soldier was tried, and though he had done nothing wicked, the judge condemned him to death. When he was led forth to die, he begged a last favor of the king.

"What is it?" asked the king.

"That I may smoke one more pipe on my way."

"You may smoke three," answered the king, "but do not imagine that I will spare your life."

Then the soldier pulled out his pipe and lighted it at the blue light, and as soon as a few wreaths of smoke had ascended, the

15) Not for nothing is the story called "The Blue Light." The soldier has to have it. Circumstances are once again dire for the soldier, and had he not been able to rely upon a fellow soldier's need for money, the hero of story would have lost the light and his own life.

16) The soldier seems to recognize that to depose a king, one must kill the bureaucracy that helps make his reign possible.

17) Happily ever after? The soldier is utterly ruthless. The king is allowed to live, but for what purpose? The princess is as badly treated as ever. No mention is made of the people who become the soldier's subjects. The soldier seems to have become as cruel as the king who dismissed him at the beginning of the tale.

little man was there with a small cudgel in his hand, and said: "What does my lord command?"

"Strike down to earth that false judge there, and his constable, and spare not the king who has treated me so ill."[16]

Then the manikin fell on them like lightning, darting this way and that way, and whosoever was so much as touched by his cudgel fell to earth, and did not venture to stir again. The king was terrified; he threw himself on the soldier's mercy, and merely to be allowed to live at all, gave him his kingdom for his own, and his daughter to wife.[17]

KING PIG

Introduction

Strolling around a county fair might lead people to believe that pigs are pretty nice. They are smart, and piglets look adorable. They relax into sleep with a snorty, snuffling ease that insomniacs would envy.

The swine barn, however, smells the worst of all the animal barns at the fair. Walking past their stalls is not for the squeamish. And if you look closely at their little eyes, they can seem full of anger and spite.

The half-man/half-pig hero of "King Pig" boasts none of the cuteness of the piglet. He is angry as an adult. He manipulates his mother shamefully and intimidates her as well. He lusts for a human bride. There is nothing restful about him. He is neither man nor pig, but a monster.

King Pig is a monster who gets a happy ending. Our hero kills two poor but beautiful sisters before he successfully marries a third, which means that "King Pig," like many other fairy tales, is a crime story. Yet, strangely, the happy ending he receives does not jar as much as it might. For King Pig is a victim at birth. He is the victim of a fairy's spite, and he cannot seem to help his nature.

Our story first appeared in Italy in the sixteenth century in a book called *The Facetious Nights of Straparola.* Straparola's work may not be well-known by average American readers, but its impact on the fairy tale genre as a whole cannot be underestimated. The sixteenth-century, two-volume collection of stories has such potent allure that one of the most beloved fairy tales of all time, "Puss in Boots," can be traced to it, as can many others, including "The Nixy," elsewhere in this book.

Precious little is known about Giovanni Francesco Straparola. He was Italian. He lived sometime in the fifteenth and sixteenth centuries. Yet he paved the way for literary fairy tales with his clever collection of stories with a framework similar to *The Decameron*. The stories are sometimes fantastic and sometimes bawdy. "King Pig" is both.

Consider:

- The conception of King Pig is odd, even by fairy tale standards. Ersilia, King Pig's mother, appears to have done nothing wrong to offend the fairies who happen upon her. She is innocently sleeping. Yet, with no provocation, and after the other two fairies have blessed the queen, the third fairy lays a horrible fate upon her. What could explain this? Is it a metaphor for the idea that life sometimes deals people inexplicable blows? Could there be some real-life context for this that was understood in the lives of the Italian upper crust, but is now lost to time? Is there anything in the story that explains this cruel blow to Ersilia?

- The names and details of this story seem unusually specific for a fairy tale. There is no evidence that the names and places mentioned in the story are saying, with accuracy, "*This* story is about *this* family (or place)." Yet the specificity may give encouragement to audiences for applying the story to real people. Take King Henry VIII of England, who lived roughly the same time as Straparola. A large man who eventually became physically repellant, not to mention obsessed with marrying and having a son, his story could be connected to King Pig's by audiences in the know about court scandals in Europe.

Or not. Still, the name and place details seem designed to encourage a kind of familiarity—the sort that breeds contempt. Notice that the story ends with everyone referring to the hero as "King Pig," despite his human form. King Pig can never forget that his subjects know all about how he started. Is the story, then, somewhat mocking about the divine right of kings? Isn't a story about a hog prince inherently critical of the fitness of royalty—at least some royalty?

- Is "King Pig" so dreadful in its details about wedding nights and murders that it is not fit to be told? The story is disturbing because it is violent, its hero wallows in "filth" (which probably means things nastier than say, garden soil), and it is unclear as to what passes between King Pig and Meldina on their wedding night.

  Not every tale gets to live on in popular imagination and culture. Based on what you've read, does "King Pig" seem too dreadful to live on? Compare it to a similar story, like "Hans My Hedge-Hog," which is less violent and more currently popular. Do the changes make the story more palatable? Or is the story simply a rather disgusting curiosity that is largely of no worth?

- Meldina and King Pig get a happily ever after. Apparently, their marriage works well. Given who the prince was for most of the story, does Meldina's attitude on the wedding night seem admirable? Does it only highlight the desperation she must have felt? Does it seem prudent or wise? Does it suggest she senses an enchantment?

- Oh, the front stories, the back stories—all the stories that could result from "King Pig." What would a story about the cursing fairy's motivation be like? How would you write Meldina? What would Ersilia's story be like? What might the fairies say after the curse is lifted? Also, note how much the traditionally significant number three appears in this story. There are three fairies who make three pronouncements, three daughters who become three brides, and Meldina has three wise sayings she follows. Could a story be made from the threes here?

KING PIG

(From the W.G. Waters translation of
The Nights of Straparola, 1894)

Fair ladies, if man were to spend a thousand years in rendering thanks to his creator for having made him in the form of a human and not of a brute beast, he could not speak gratitude enough.[1] This reflection calls to mind the story of one who was born as a pig, but afterwards became a comely youth. Nevertheless, to his dying day he was known to the people over whom he ruled as King Pig.

You must know, dear ladies, that Galeotto, King of Anglia, was a man highly blest in worldly riches, and in his wife Ersilia, the daughter of Matthias, King of Hungary, a princess who, in virtue and beauty, outshone all the other ladies of the time.[2] And Galeotto was a wise king, ruling his land so that no man could hear complaint against him. Though they had been several years married they had no child, wherefore they both of them were much aggrieved.

While Ersilia was walking one day in her garden she felt suddenly weary, and noticing a nearby spot covered with fresh

1) *Addressing the "fair ladies" is part of the set up for the "Facetious Nights," which also involves women telling the stories.*

2) *The amount of specific naming is intriguing. It could be done to deliberately cause confusion about the real subjects of the story, it could just be detail for detail's sake or it could be a pastiche of names for people and places used to give the tale a once-upon-a-time feeling. Or maybe the amount of naming that takes place is designed to encourage the audience to supply specific names on their own to make the tale extra personal and gossipy. Naming has power.*

3) Much-wished-for pregnancies are often magically brought about in natural settings, like gardens. The parents of Rapunzel desperately want a child, for example, and the baby's birth is connected to the forbidden walled garden they live next to. Snow White's mother longs for a child as she contemplates snow through a window.

4) Fairies are often shown to be spiteful in folklore, but the third fairy's ill-wishing is notably cruel. The fig leaf of a forgotten invitation to a christening, as in "Sleeping Beauty," is not even offered here. Although the narrator tells us that these fairies were known to have contempt for humans, this doesn't fully explain the depth of the third fairy's cruelty. Unless the message here is that cruelty cannot always be understood. Also, the third fairy may be the most powerful.

green turf, she went up to it and sat down thereon, and, overcome with weariness and soothed by the sweet singing of the birds in the green foliage, she fell asleep.[3]

And it chanced that while she slept there passed by three fairies who held mankind somewhat in scorn, and these, when they beheld the sleeping queen, halted, and gazing upon her beauty, took counsel together how they might protect her and throw a spell upon her.

When they were agreed, the first cried out, "I will that no man shall be able to harm her, and that, the next time she lie with her husband, she may be with child and bear a son who shall not have his equal in all the world for beauty."

Then said the second, "I will that no one shall ever have power to offend her, and that the prince who shall be born of her shall be gifted with every virtue under the sun."

And the third said, "And I will that she shall be the wisest among women, but that the son whom she shall conceive shall be born in the skin of a pig, with a pig's ways and manners, and in this state he shall be constrained to abide till he shall have three times taken a woman to wife."[4]

As soon as the three fairies had flown away Ersilia awoke, and straightway arose and went back to the palace, taking with her the flowers she had plucked. Not many days had passed before she knew herself to be with child, and when the time of her delivery was come, she gave birth to a son with members like those of a pig and not of a human being.[5]

When tidings of this prodigy came to the ears of the king and queen they lamented sore, and the king, bearing in mind how good and wise his queen was, often felt moved to put this offspring of hers to death and cast it into the sea, in order that she might be spared the shame of having given birth to him. But when he debated in his mind and considered that this son, let him be what he might, was of his own begetting, he put aside the cruel purpose which he had been harboring, and, seized with pity and grief, he made up his mind that the son should be brought up and nurtured like a rational being and not as a brute beast.[6]

The child, therefore, being nursed with the greatest care, would often be brought to the queen and put his little snout and his little paws in his mother's lap, and she, moved by natural affection, would caress him by stroking his bristly back with her hand, and embracing and kissing him as if he had been of human form. Then he would wag his tail and give other signs to show that he was conscious of his mother's affection.[7]

The pigling, when he grew older, began

5) "Members," in this case, appears to apply to the prince's nose, feet, etc.

6) The king's dilemma is understandable. As much as parents love their children, Galeotto and Ersilia are in an unusual situation, even by fairy-tale standards. It is possible that the narrator is hinting that allowing the pig prince to live in the first place was an act of stupid indulgence of the parents' part. Fairy tales are not famous for approval of human ugliness.

7) Ersilia's tenderness for her son will bring her to grief, as she is faced with his increasingly brutal demands. She may be destined for wisdom, according to the third fairy's decree, but at quite a cost.

8) King Pig's demand is outrageous and unnatural to anyone who is not a pig prince. Even his own mother is outraged. Were she too easily accepting of her son's request, she might lose the audience's sympathy.

9) A rhetorical question, apparently.

to talk like a human being, and to wander abroad in the city, but whenever he came near to any mud or dirt he would always wallow therein, after the manner of pigs, and return all covered with filth. Then, when he approached the king and queen, he would rub his sides against their fair garments, defiling them with all manner of dirt, but because he was indeed their own son they bore it all.

One day he came home covered with mud and filth, as was his wont, and lay down on his mother's rich robe, and said in a grunting tone, "Mother, I wish to get married."

When the queen heard this, she replied, "Do not talk so foolishly. What maid would ever take you for a husband, and think you that any noble or knight would give his daughter to one so dirty and ill-savored as you?"[8]

But he kept on grunting that he must have a wife of one sort or another. The queen, not knowing how to manage him in this matter, asked the king what they should do in their trouble, "Our son wishes to marry, but where shall we find anyone who will take him as a husband?"[9]

Every day the pig would come back to his mother with the same demand, "I must have a wife, and I will never leave you in peace until you procure for me a certain maiden I have seen today, who pleases me greatly."

It happened that this maiden was a daughter of a poor woman who had three daughters. When the queen heard this, she had brought before her the poor woman and her eldest daughter, and said, "Good mother, you are poor and burdened with children. If you will agree to what I shall say to you, you will be rich. I have this son who is, as you see, in form a pig, and I would fain marry him to your eldest daughter. Do not consider him, but think of the king and of me, and remember that your daughter will inherit this whole kingdom when the king and I shall be dead."[10]

When the young girl listened to the words of the queen she was greatly disturbed in her mind and blushed red for shame, and then said that on no account would she listen to the queen's proposition; but the poor mother besought her so pressingly that at last she yielded.

When the pig came home one day, all covered with dirt as usual, his mother said to him, "My son, we have found for you the wife you desire." And then she caused to be brought in the bride, who by this time had been robed in sumptuous regal attire, and presented her to the pig prince. When he saw how lovely and desirable she was he was filled with joy, and, all foul and

10) Approaching a poor mother may be practical on Ersilia's part, but it also reminds us of how easily rich and powerful people exploit the poor. Also, this part of the story marks the beginning of a long stretch of bad parenting in "King Pig." Ersilia, through love and fear, gives into her son's demands and the mother of the three poor sisters sells them as brides to a pig. Even taking her desperation into account, after the pig prince kills the first sister, it would seem prudent for the mothers to refuse any further marriages. Both she and Ersilia make bad parenting decisions. Yet, the king, who not only is the head of his family, but the country as well, has largely disappeared from the story. His marked absence may be a critique of his weak character, and, implicitly, the character of actual kings.

123

11) The first wife's fears about her clothes seem designed to make her unsympathetic, as vanity is one of the Seven Deadly Sins. Yet, clearly, before the marriage, she was rightfully horrified at the prospect of marrying a pig-man.

12) It seems it's kill or be killed for King Pig, but does this make what comes next justifiable?

13) "He lay down by his spouse, who was not long in falling to sleep, and then he struck her with his sharp hoofs and drove them into her breast so that he killed her." This sentence is one of the most memorable in the whole story. It seems an unusually cruel (and slow) way to kill someone. There is an intimacy to the act that is deeply disturbing.

dirty as he was, jumped round about her, endeavoring by his pawing and nuzzling to show some sign of his affection.

But she, when she found he was soiling her beautiful dress, thrust him aside; whereupon the pig said to her, "Why do you push me thus? Have I not had these garments made for you myself?"[11]

Then she answered disdainfully, "No, neither you nor any other of the whole kingdom of hogs has done this thing."

And when the time for going to bed was come the young girl said to herself, "What am I to do with this foul beast? This very night, while he lies in his first sleep, I will kill him."[12]

The pig prince, who was not far off, heard these words, but said nothing, and when the two retired to their chamber he got into the bed, stinking and dirty as he was, and defiled the sumptuous bed with his filthy paws and snout. He lay down by his spouse, who was not long in falling to sleep, and then he struck her with his sharp hoofs and drove them into her breast so that he killed her.[13]

The next morning the queen went to visit her daughter-in-law, and to her great grief found that the pig had killed her; and when he came back from wandering about the city he said, in reply to the queen's bitter reproaches, that he had only wrought with his wife as she was minded to deal with him, and then withdrew in an ill humor.

Not many days had passed before the pig prince again began to beseech the queen to allow him to marry one of the other sisters, and because the queen at first would not listen to his petition he persisted in his purpose, and threatened to ruin everything in the palace if he could not have her to wife. The queen, when she heard this, went to the king and told him everything, and he made answer that perhaps it would be wiser to kill their ill-fated offspring before he might work some fatal mischief in the city.[14]

But the queen felt all the tenderness of a mother toward him, and loved him very dearly in spite of his brutal person, and could not endure the thought of being parted from him; so she summoned once more to the palace the poor woman, together with her second daughter, and held a long discourse with her, begging her all the while to give her daughter in marriage.[15]

At last the girl assented to take the pig prince for a husband; but her fate was no happier than her sister's, for the bridegroom killed her, as he had killed his other bride, and then fled headlong from the palace.

When he came back dirty as usual and smelling so foully that no one could

14) *Although the king is not very much in evidence for much of this story, his willingness to sacrifice his son shows he is aware of his responsibility to his subjects—including potential daughters-in-law. On the other hand, he knows he is safe. Ersilia will never agree to kill their son.*

15) *Although the third fairy, who also cursed her, said Ersilia would become wise, evidence of wisdom is thin on the ground at this point. Although she clearly knows that she may be sacrificing another girl's life to fulfill her son's desires, she nonetheless procures another bride for him. In addition, once again, the poor mother agrees to sacrifice a daughter to the pig prince.*

16) The prince's demands
have escalated to the
point that he is
threatening his own
mother. He is at the
height of his beastliness,
seemingly beyond hope or
redemption.

approach him, the king and queen censured him gravely for the outrage he had wrought; but again he cried out boldly that if he had not killed her she would have killed him.

As it had happened before, the pig in a very short time began to importune his mother again to let him have to wife the youngest sister, who was much more beautiful than either of the others; and when this request of his was refused steadily, he became more insistent than ever, and in the end began to threaten the queen's life in violent and bloodthirsty words, unless he should have given to him the young girl for his wife.[16]

The queen, when she heard this shameful and unnatural speech, was well-nigh broken hearted and like to go out of her mind; but, putting all other considerations aside, she called for the poor woman and her third daughter, who was named Meldina, and thus addressed her, "Meldina, my child, I should be greatly pleased if you would take the pig prince for a husband; pay no regard to him, but to his father and to me; then, if you will be prudent and bear patiently with him, you may be the happiest woman in the world."

To this speech Meldina answered, with a grateful smile upon her face, that she was quite content to do as the queen bade her, and thanked her humbly for deigning to choose her as a daughter-in-law; for, seeing that she herself had nothing in the world, it was indeed great good fortune that she, a poor girl, should become the daughter-in-law of a potent sovereign.[17]

The queen, when she heard this modest and amiable reply, could not keep back her tears for the happiness she felt; but she feared all the time that the same fate might be in store for Meldina as her sisters.

When the new bride had been clothed in rich attire and decked with jewels, and was awaiting the bridegroom, the pig prince came in, filthier and more muddy than ever; but she spread out her rich gown and besought him to lie down by her side. Whereupon the queen bade her to thrust him away, but to this she would not consent, and spoke thus to the queen, "There are three wise sayings, gracious lady, which I remember to have heard. The first is that it is folly to waste time in searching for that which cannot be found. The second is that we should believe nothing we may hear, except those things which bear the marks of sense and reason. The third is that, when once you have got possession of some rare and precious treasure, prize it well and keep a firm hold upon it."[18]

When the maiden had finished speaking, the pig prince, who had been

17) *Meldina shows astonishing self-possession in the face of a fate that would drive most women to hysteria or murder—as her first sister contemplated. Could it be that she senses enchantment?*

18) *Meldina embraces her fate in a docile, positive way. Her words suggest that she knows she cannot avoid life with the prince and that she needs to think for herself.*

19) *Just what happens and will happen between Meldina and the prince is shrouded in vague wording. Certainly, the fact that Meldina is enthusiastically accepting of the kisses and touch of a pig-man is shocking enough. This part of the story may also explain why it is not widely read today.*

20) *Meldina's acceptance of her fate continues to be startling. Again, one wonders if she senses that the prince may be more and better than he seems.*

21) *The prince has labored with a secret as well as a curse. Is the dual nature of his existence behind his anger? Or did being a pig prince simply give him a beastly nature?*

wide awake and had heard all that she had said, got up, kissed her on the face and neck and bosom and shoulders with his tongue, and she was not backward in returning his caresses; so that he was fired with a warm love for her.[19]

As soon as the time for retiring for the night had come, the bride went to bed and awaited her unseemly spouse, and, as soon as he came, she raised the coverlet and bade him lie near to her and put his head upon the pillow, covering him carefully with the bedclothes and drawing the curtains so that he might feel no cold.

When morning had come the pig got up and ranged abroad to pasture, as was his wont, and very soon after the queen went to the bride's chamber, expecting to find that she had met with the same fate as her sisters; but when she saw her lying in the bed, all defiled with mud as it was, and looking pleased and contented, she thanked God for this favor, that her son had at last found a spouse according to his liking.[20]

One day, soon after this, when the pig prince was conversing pleasantly with his wife, he said to her, "Meldina, my beloved wife, if I could be fully sure that you could keep a secret, I would now tell you one of mine; something I have kept hidden for many years. I know you to be very prudent and wise, and that you love me truly; so I wish to make you the sharer of my secret."[21]

"You may safely tell it to me, if you will," said Meldina, "for I promise never to reveal it to anyone without your consent."

Whereupon, being now sure of his wife's discretion and fidelity, he straightaway shook off from his body the foul and dirty skin of the pig, and stood revealed as a handsome and well shaped young man, and all that night rested closely folded in the arms of his beloved wife.[22]

But he charged her solemnly to keep silence about this wonder she had seen, for the time had not yet come for his complete delivery from this misery. So when he left the bed he donned the dirty pig's hide once more. I leave you to imagine for yourselves how great was the great joy of Meldina when she discovered that, instead of a pig, she had gained a handsome and gallant young prince for a husband.

Not long after this she proved to be with child, and when the time her delivery came she gave birth to a fair and shapely boy. The joy of the king and queen was unbounded, especially when they found that the newborn child had the form of a human being and not that of a beast.[23]

But the burden of the strange and weighty secret which her husband had confided to her pressed heavily upon

22) *Animal bridegrooms who live as humans at night can be traced back to the story of Cupid and Psyche, from 2,000 years ago. "East of the Sun, West of the Moon," the well-known Scandinavian tale, features a prince who is a bear by day and a beautiful man at night.*

23) *It seems that the arrival of a fully human baby would tip everyone off about the possibility of enchantment where the prince is concerned. Also, why would they assume the prince's baby would have any pig in him, unless they think Ersilia was defiled by a pig herself, resulting in the birth of her porcine son?*

24) *Meldina, like other heroines in animal bridegroom stories, eventually cannot keep the secret of her husband's humanity. Usually, this portends a long journey for the blabbing bride.*

Meldina, and one day she went to her mother-in-law and said, "Gracious queen, when first I married your son I believed I was married to a beast, but now I find that you have given me the comeliest, the worthiest, and the most gallant young man ever born into the world to be my husband. For know that when he comes into my chamber to lie by my side, he casts off his dirty hide and leaves it on the ground, and is changed into a graceful handsome youth. No one could believe this marvel save they saw it with their own eyes."[24]

When the queen heard these words she deemed that her daughter-in-law must be jesting with her, but Meldina still persisted that what she said was true. And when the queen demanded to know how she might witness with her own eyes the truth of this thing, Meldina replied, "Come to my chamber tonight, when we shall be in our first sleep; the door will be open, and you will find that what I tell you is the truth."

That same night, when the looked-for time had come, and all were gone to rest, the queen let some torches be kindled and went, accompanied by the king, to the chamber of her son, and when she had entered she saw the pig's skin lying on the floor in the corner of the room, and having gone to the bedside, found therein a handsome young man in whose arms Meldina was lying. And when they saw this, the delight of the king and queen was very great, and the king gave order that before anyone should leave the chamber the pig's hide should be torn to shreds. So great was their joy over the recovery of their son that they well-nigh died thereof.[25]

And King Galeotto, when he saw that he had so fine a son, and a grandchild likewise, laid aside his diadem and his royal robes, and advanced to his place his son, whom he let be crowned with the greatest pomp, and who was ever afterwards known as King Pig. Thus, to the great contentment of all the people, the young king began his reign, and he lived long and happily with Meldina his beloved wife.[26]

25) *Spying on the sleeping enchanted prince in other stories of this kind is usually done by the wife at the behest of a member of her family. In this case, the pig prince's parents do it. They also quickly destroy his hide. Perhaps the fact that his parents are spying makes their actions acceptable—there will be no journey of atonement for Meldina. Only happiness.*

26) *No matter how well he does or how high he rises or how beloved he is, King Pig will never be allowed to forget his roots. The name of "King Pig" shows affection, but it's affection with a barb tucked inside.*

KISA THE CAT

Introduction

Friendship is not often the focus of fairy tales, although good companionship is celebrated. For example, "The Bremen Town Musicians" clearly celebrates companionship, not to mention the importance of community in one's declining years. "The Three Pennies," a grateful dead story in this book, features a friendly relationship between man and ghost. Fairy tales are so numerous and varied that eventually almost all human behavior is addressed in them, even friendship. "Kisa the Cat," an Icelandic fairy tale most commonly found in Andrew Lang's *The Brown Fairy Book* (1904), features a cat who is both a powerful helper, like Puss from "Puss in Boots," and a friend and companion to Ingibjorg, the main princess in the story.

Cats are fairly common in fairy tales. Besides Kisa and Puss, there is the marvelous tale "The White Cat," by Madame d'Aulnoy; "King of the Cats," an English folk story; and "Dick Whittington and His Cat," also English. Although cats sometimes were viewed with suspicion because of their association with witches, in fairy tales they are usually portrayed as the clever, resourceful, brave creatures they actually are.

Kisa is the brains in this story. She not only is brave and clever, she can drive a pony cart, and, apparently, can use her paws like hands, plus is an expert in healing with magic and herbs. Ingibjorg is rather spoiled and, while not unpleasant, is clearly playing second fiddle to Kisa in every way. It's not surprising to find out that Kisa has been under enchantment, as we do at the end of the story.

Princes are found at the end of the story, for both Kisa and Ingibjorg, but they are more accessories than men in this tale. The friendship between a girl and her faithful cat is what matters in this story, reminding us that romantic relationships are not always the focus of fairy tales. Instead, friendship formed in childhood is celebrated here.

Consider:

- The yearning for a child opens up this fairy tale, as it does so many others. "Snow White," "Sleeping Beauty," and "King Pig" all open with a wish for a child, as does "Thumbelina." Given that desire for a child is often followed by great trouble in these tales, is disapproval for wanting a child too much implied? Or, do the tales help illustrate the deep pain infertility causes? Both? Perhaps magical intervention is an issue in the tales where it is found. Magic almost always has a price, in any story. Do the passionately-hoped-for offspring pay the price for the magical acts that beget them?

- The power in this tales lies with the enchanted cats. Both Kisa and her mother seem to be extraordinary creatures. Given that cats were often viewed with suspicion in times gone by, what explains the powerfully positive status of cats in tales like this one? Can you think of other tales that feature animals ordinarily viewed with disdain possessing power and strength? Which tales are they? How do they relate to "Kisa the Cat"? What do the tales lead you to conclude about the status of animals in fairy tales? In our time, animals are increasingly viewed as vital creatures with their own rights. Yet do these tales suggest that taking animals seriously is not a new idea at all?

- Kisa's willingness to help Ingibjorg stems from her desire to free herself from enchantment. Yet her attitude toward the princess is as kindly as her actions. Self interest is not her only motivation. What explains her gentleness with Ingibjorg? Is it a way to communicate her essential goodness? Or, is it possibly connected to the spell that Kisa was under? Kisa says that she and her mother were enchanted by a "spiteful fairy," but is it possible the enchanted women caused the spite themselves? What do fairy tales tell us about rousing the ire of powerful fairies?

- Does the fact that Kisa spends time in the princess's bed at the beginning of the tale and at the end matter at all? Is it meant to signify how close they were, like sisters? (People of all stations often slept in the same bed in days gone by, including the highborn and their servants.) Is it just a detail? Can you think of any other tales in which characters' sleeping in the same bed may be an important detail? Can they be related to this tale? If so, how, and does the relationship matter significantly in understanding and interpreting the tales?

- "Kisa the Cat" just begs for back stories and post-happily-ever-after tales. Do Ingibjorg and Kisa remain best friends forever? What did cause the fairies' spite? What is Ingibjorg's prince like? What about the giant and his wife? Just because he is "horrible" doesn't mean he doesn't deserve a story. Also, what do Kisa (as a cat and after) and Ingibjorg look like? Does it matter?

KISA THE CAT.

(By Andrew Lang, from The Brown Fairy Book, 1904)

Once upon a time there lived a queen who had a beautiful cat, the color of smoke, with china-blue eyes, which she was very fond of. The cat was constantly with her, and ran after her wherever she went, and even sat up proudly by her side when she drove out in her fine glass coach.[1]

"Oh, pussy," said the queen one day, "you are happier than I am! For you have a dear kitten just like yourself, and I have nobody to play with but you."

"Don't cry," answered the cat, laying her paw on her mistress's arm. "Crying never does any good. I will see what can be done."

The cat was as good as her word. As soon as she returned from her drive she trotted off to the forest to consult a fairy who dwelt there, and very soon after the queen had a little girl, who seemed made out of snow and sunbeams.[2] The queen was delighted, and soon the baby began to take notice of the kitten as she jumped about the room, and would not go to sleep at all unless the kitten lay curled up beside her.[3]

1) *The glass coach mentioned here probably isn't made mostly of glass. Instead, it probably is a coach with windows, which were pretty high end. The term may also be referencing The Glass Coach used by Britain's royal family. It has been in use since the late 19th century.†*

2) *Although fairy gifts are often of dubious value, in this case, little Ingibjorg seems to have had a touch of magic added to her appearance. The description "snow and sunbeams" is fanciful indeed.*

3) *Kisa and her mother are essential to the very existence of Ingibjorg. Kisa is so important to the princess from the beginning of the story that it's amazing the child thrives without her for a number of years. Then*

(cont.) again, we do need a reason for the story's action.

4) *We never do find out why Kisa disappears. Ingibjorg herself raises the issue, but events intervene and we never know why Kisa left. This may be a deliberate attempt to leave the reader with interesting questions to ponder. It may be an oversight. It may be that Lang, in writing his adaptation from the Icelandic tale, did not think the question worth answering, as he had other elements to wrangle.*

Two or three months went by, and though the baby was still a baby, the kitten was fast becoming a cat, and one evening when, as usual, the nurse came to look for her, to put her in the baby's cot, she was nowhere to be found. What a hunt there was for that kitten, to be sure! The servants, each anxious to find her, as the queen was certain to reward the lucky man, searched in the most impossible places. Boxes were opened that would hardly have held the kitten's paw; books were taken from bookshelves, lest the kitten should have got behind them, drawers were pulled out, for perhaps the kitten might have got shut in. But it was all no use. The kitten had plainly run away, and nobody could tell if it would ever choose to come back.[4]

Years passed away, and one day, when the princess was playing ball in the garden, she happened to throw her ball farther than usual, and it fell into a clump of rose-bushes. The princess of course ran after it at once, and she was stooping down to feel if it was hidden in the long grass, when she heard a voice calling her: "Ingibjorg! Ingibjorg!" it said, "have you forgotten me? I am Kisa, your sister!"

"But I never HAD a sister," answered Ingibjorg, very much puzzled; for she knew nothing of what had taken place so long ago.

"Don't you remember how I always slept in your cot beside you, and how you cried till I came? But girls have no memories at all! Why, I could find my way straight up to that cot this moment, if I was once inside the palace."

"Why did you go away then?" asked the princess. But before Kisa could answer, Ingibjorg's attendants arrived breathless on the scene, and were so horrified at the sight of a strange cat, that Kisa plunged into the bushes and went back to the forest.[5]

The princess was very much vexed with her ladies-in-waiting for frightening away her old playfellow, and told the queen who came to her room every evening to bid her good-night.

"Yes, it is quite true what Kisa said," answered the queen; "I should have liked to see her again. Perhaps, some day, she will return, and then you must bring her to me."

Next morning it was very hot, and the princess declared that she must go and play in the forest, where it was always cool, under the big shady trees. As usual, her attendants let her do anything she pleased, and sitting down on a mossy bank where a little stream tinkled by, soon fell sound asleep. The princess saw with delight that they would pay no heed to her, and wandered on and on, expecting every moment to see some fairies dancing round a ring, or some little

5) *The servants' horror at the cat is hard to understand. It's clear that cats have had a powerful place at this court. But servants' failures are part of the fairy tale tradition. Remember that in the Grimms' "Snow White," she only comes out of her deathlike sleep because servants stumble with her coffin while carrying her down a mountain.*

6) Ingibjorg does not have her finest hour in this paragraph. She is shown to be both spoiled rotten and willing to follow a giant into danger because he tells her so. What would Kisa do?

7) Very bad things happen to children in fairy tales. Sometimes, a child commits an alleged sin and receives harsh punishment—like Karen's vanity in Andersen's "The Red Shoes." Interestingly, she also has her feet chopped off. Unlike Karen, however, Ingibjorg does not appear to have lost her feet for any real or perceived sins.

brown elves peeping at her from behind a tree. But, alas! she met none of these; instead, a horrible giant came out of his cave and ordered her to follow him. The princess felt much afraid, as he was so big and ugly, and began to be sorry that she had not stayed within reach of help; but as there was no use in disobeying the giant, she walked meekly behind.[6]

They went a long way, and Ingibjorg grew very tired, and at length began to cry.

"I don't like girls who make horrid noises," said the giant, turning round. "But if you WANT to cry, I will give you something to cry for." And drawing an axe from his belt, he cut off both her feet, which he picked up and put in his pocket. Then he went away.[7]

Poor Ingibjorg lay on the grass in terrible pain, and wondering if she should stay there till she died, as no one would know where to look for her. How long it was since she had set out in the morning she could not tell—it seemed years to her, of course; but the sun was still high in the heavens when she heard the sound of wheels, and then, with a great effort, for her throat was parched with fright and pain, she gave a shout.

"I am coming!" was the answer; and in another moment a cart made its way through the trees, driven by Kisa, who used her tail as a whip to urge the horse to go faster. Directly Kisa saw Ingibjorg lying there, she jumped quickly down, and lifting the girl carefully in her two front paws, laid her upon some soft hay, and drove back to her own little hut.

In the corner of the room was a pile of cushions, and these Kisa arranged as a bed. Ingibjorg, who by this time was nearly fainting from all she had gone through, drank greedily some milk, and then sank back on the cushions while Kisa fetched some dried herbs from a cupboard, soaked them in warm water and tied them on the bleeding legs. The pain vanished at once, and Ingibjorg looked up and smiled at Kisa.[8]

"You will go to sleep now," said the cat, "and you will not mind if I leave you for a little while. I will lock the door, and no one can hurt you." But before she had finished the princess was asleep. Then Kisa got into the cart, which was standing at the door, and catching up the reins, drove straight to the giant's cave.

Leaving her cart behind some trees, Kisa crept gently up to the open door, and, crouching down, listened to what the giant was telling his wife, who was at supper with him.

"The first day that I can spare I shall just go back and kill her," he said; "it would never do for people in the forest to know that a mere girl can defy me!" And he and his wife were so busy calling Ingibjorg all sorts of names for her bad behavior, that

8) *Kisa shows herself to be sensitive and thoughtful in this passage. She doesn't just ease her charge's pain, she makes her comfortable. While Kisa needs to be kind in order to be free of enchantment, these small graces seem to be the result of true affection for Ingibjorg.*

9) *Kisa's bravery, stealth, and cunning may be part of her half-human/half-cat nature. It seems she is possessed of the best qualities of both species. Also, in pointing out the spiteful conversation the giant and his wife were having, Lang reminds us that loose talk and meanness break focus and make us vulnerable.*

10) *Kisa wastes no time on retribution or looking for treasure. She's like a modern-day medical professional. Get those feet reattached, stat!*

11) *The princess, apparently, did not sleep very long. Also, those "neat little feet" in silver slippers seem pretty gruesome.*

they never noticed Kisa stealing into a dark corner, and upsetting a whole bag of salt into the great pot before the fire.[9]

"Dear me, how thirsty I am!" cried the giant by-and-by.

"So am I," answered the wife. "I do wish I had not taken that last spoonful of broth; I am sure something was wrong with it."

"If I don't get some water I shall die," went on the giant. And rushing out of the cave, followed by his wife, he ran down the path which led to the river.

Then Kisa entered the hut, and lost no time in searching every hole till she came upon some grass, under which Ingibjorg's feet were hidden, and putting them in her cart, drove back again to her own hut.[10]

Ingibjorg was thankful to see her, for she had lain, too frightened to sleep, trembling at every noise.

"Oh, is it you?" she cried joyfully, as Kisa turned the key. And the cat came in, holding up the two neat little feet in their silver slippers.[11]

"In two minutes they shall be as tight as they ever were!" said Kisa. And taking some strings of the magic grass which the giant had carelessly heaped on them, she bound the feet on to the legs above.

"Of course you won't be able to walk for some time; you must not expect THAT," she continued. "But if you are very good, perhaps, in about a week, I may carry you home again."[12]

And so she did; and when the cat drove the cart up to the palace gate, lashing the horse furiously with her tail, and the king and queen saw their lost daughter sitting beside her, they declared that no reward could be too great for the person who had brought her out of the giant's hands.

"We will talk about that by-and-by," said the cat, as she made her best bow, and turned her horse's head.

The princess was very unhappy when Kisa left her without even bidding her farewell.[13] She would neither eat nor drink, nor take any notice of all the beautiful dresses her parents bought for her.

"She will die, unless we can make her laugh," one whispered to the other. "Is there anything in the world that we have left untried?"

"Nothing except marriage," answered the king.[14] And he invited all the handsomest young men he could think of to the palace, and bade the princess choose a husband from among them.

It took her some time to decide which she admired the most, but at last she fixed upon a young prince, whose eyes were like the pools in the forest, and his hair of bright gold. The king and the queen were greatly pleased, as the young man was the son of a

12) Kisa has taken on the persona of an older, loving sister, who will scold and gently bully Ingibjorg for her own good. Kisa's words remind us that she is older and wiser than Ingibjorg.

13) Why Kisa leaves again is unclear. Perhaps she knows that if she stays, the princess will not end up married, as Ingibjorg would be content with Kisa.

14) That'll cure her!

15) *Since Kisa arrives and cheers Ingibjorg up, we'll never know if marriage really would have helped the latter's state of mind.*

16) *The newlywed prince must have felt lucky indeed. He lies down with a wife and a cat and wakes up with two beautiful women.*

17) *The friendship between Kisa and Ingibjorg remains central to the story. The princes are window dressing. The happily ever after is for the two princesses.*

neighboring king, and they gave orders that a splendid feast should be got ready.

When the marriage was over, Kisa suddenly stood before them, and Ingibjorg rushed forward and clasped her in her arms.[15]

"I have come to claim my reward," said the cat. "Let me sleep for this night at the foot of your bed."

"Is that ALL?" asked Ingibjorg, much disappointed.

"It is enough," answered the cat. And when the morning dawned, it was no cat that lay upon the bed, but a beautiful princess.[16]

"My mother and I were both enchanted by a spiteful fairy," said she, "we could not free ourselves till we had done some kindly deed that had never been wrought before. My mother died without ever finding a chance of doing anything new, but I took advantage of the evil act of the giant to make you as whole as ever."

Then they were all more delighted than before, and the princess lived in the court until she, too, married, and went away to govern one of her own.[17]

Source Note

† Royal Household. "Carriages." *The Official Website of the British Monarchy.*

ANNOTATED BIBLIOGRAPHY

Picking books and websites for this list was as hard as trying to pick a favorite song. I admire the work of countless writers, site managers, and bloggers. All of the following sources offer a wide variety of web links and bibliographic entries that will lead you to even more outstanding sources.

ArtMagick: Your Source of Visual Intoxication.
http://artmagick.com.

"Exquisite" is the only word to describe this site, which features plenty of nineteenth-century artwork and images from other periods as well. The Pre-Raphaelites are especially prominent and fairy tale illustration is there as well. Many paintings are not directly related to books, but paintings featuring fairy tale scenes or scenes from myths and folklore are on the site. Be prepared to lose hours of time staring at the loveliest images you may ever find outside a museum.

Brasey, Edouard, Brigitte Leblanc, Sabine Houplain, and Florence Brutton. *Faeries and Demons: And Other Magical Creatures*. New York: Barnes & Noble, 2003.

Faeries and Demons is gorgeous. Less a reference book than a reverie on the charms and perils of an enchanted and enchanting world, the book is divided by holidays of the four seasons. Despite its emphasis on whimsy, the book does include some useful ideas about the fairy world, and is great fun to read. It's impossible to overstate how much fun this book is to look through.

Cabinet des Fees. http://www.cabinetdesfees.com.

Cabinet des Fees is packed with stories, poems, reviews, essays, and art about fairy tales and folklore. The site is well organized, allowing visitors to navigate its many offerings easily. It's a great place for writers and poets who are inspired by fairy tales, plus scholars, readers, and anyone who enjoys fantasy.

Cashdan, Sheldon. *The Witch Must Die: How Fairy Tales Shape Our Lives*. New York, NY: Basic Books, 1999.

Cashdan's popular work on fairy tales brings insight to classic stories using a psychological point of view. His use of the Seven Deadly Sins to provide a framework for his assertions makes the book especially accessible for the everyday reader. He also provides provocative ideas about *The Wizard of Oz* and Disney. A highly readable work and a major research favorite for students in my fairy tale classes.

D.L. Ashliman's Home Page. http://www.pitt.edu/~dash/ashliman.html

Don't let the utilitarian name and look of this website fool you, D.L. Ashliman's collection of fairy tales and folklore is thoughtfully organized, amazingly wide-ranging and essential to fairy tale and folklore studies. Ashliman, a noted folklore scholar and translator, provides an especially comprehensive array of Brothers Grimm tales. Links to a huge number of fairy tale and folklore sites are there, and there are even links to sites in other languages.

Enchanted Conversation: A Fairy Tale Magazine. http://www.fairytalemagazine.com.

Enchanted Conversation is a blog and a 'zine that features stories and poems that provide new takes on specific classic fairy tales and works that are influenced by fairy tales and folklore. Non-fiction works about all aspects of fairy tales are also regularly featured, through my posts and many guest posts. I am editor and publisher of *Enchanted Conversation*. The site will feature a special section focused on discussing *Beyond the Glass Slipper*. *Enchanted Conversation* is an outgrowth of Diamondsandtoads.com, a site that is now managed by Tahlia Merrill.

von Franz, Marie-Luise. *The Interpretation of Fairy Tales.* Rev. ed. Boston: Shambhala, 1996.

A highly influential book that focuses on archetypes to explore the import and use of fairy tales, *The Interpretation of Fairy Tales* challenges the reader about fairy tales and their impact and intersection with the collective unconscious. "The Three

Feathers," a Brothers Grimm tale, is a focal point for von Franz's explorations. The author, who died in 1998, was a major figure in the field of Jungian psychology.

Haase, Donald, ed. *The Greenwood Encyclopedia of Folktales and Fairy Tales.* **Westport, Conn.: Greenwood Press, 2008.**

Types of fairy tales and folklore, information on well-known fairy tale writers and scholars, famous illustrators, movies, schools of criticism—you name it, you may very well be able to find it in these three volumes. Students especially enjoy this resource. The set is expensive, so see if your library has it available.

The Journal of Mythic Arts. http://endicottstudio.typepad.com.

A sad sigh went 'round the world of fairy tale lovers when *The Journal of Mythic Arts* ceased publication in 2008. Luckily for us, the archives remain available, and what a site. As a source for learning and thinking about fairy tales, JoMA is second to none. Thoughtfully edited, well focused, yet comprehensive, scholars and fairy tale fans alike will find non-fiction, fiction, art (many media), and more, at JoMA. The journal was an outgrowth of Endicott Studio, which also has a site, linked to on JoMA.

Rose, Carol. *Spirits, Fairies, Leprechauns, and Goblins: An Encyclopedia.* **New York, N.Y.: Norton, 1998.**

Rose's highly detailed, but easily readable encyclopedia of all things that lurk under mushrooms, hide in the water and walk the hills, is a must-read for anyone interested in fairy tales, folklore, and the world of faerie. Heavily researched, well documented, and almost overwhelming in its variety, Rose's encyclopedia is both practical for scholars and perfect for the casual reader. If you've ever wondered how varied elves, goblins and dwarfs might be, this is the book for you.

SurLaLune Fairy Tales. http://www.surlalunefairytales.com

Perhaps the most popular fairy-tale site on the web, *SurLaLune Fairy Tales* is packed with numerous annotated fairy tales and countless illustrations. Even more fairy tales, not annotated, are available as well. Students thoroughly enjoy the site and find it easy to navigate. The site's blog, which is linked to at the site, is filled with information and news about fairy tales. Visit it once and you'll keep going back.

Tatar, Maria, ed. *The Annotated Classic Fairy Tales*. New York: Norton, 2002.

The book that started my journey into using fairy tales in my writing classes, *The Annotated Classic Fairy Tales* is both beautiful and useful. Tales like "Snow White," "Bluebeard," "Sleeping Beauty," and "Beauty and the Beast" are featured here, as are somewhat lesser-known stories like "Molly Whuppie." Brief biographies of fairy tale collectors and writers as well as classic illustrators are provided as well. Tatar's annotations are the most fascinating and informative part of this book, however. Students and everyday readers will find the book enjoyable and practical for research. (Note: Tatar is also the story translator for *The Annotated Classic Fairy Tales*.)

————, ed. *The Classic Fairy Tales*. New York: Norton, 1999.

The Classic Fairy Tales is the main text for my fairy-tale writing classes because it offers a variety of fairy tales, comprehensive introductions by Tatar, and an excellent set of critical essays from fairy tale scholars. Marina Warner, Jack Zipes, Bruno Bettelheim, and a number of other luminaries in the field are featured in the essay section. In addition, both the Aarne-Thompson and Propp fairy tale and folklore classification systems are available. Instructors at both the college and high-school levels could build a course around this book, but the casual reader would enjoy *The Classic Fairy Tales* as well.

Zipes, Jack. *Breaking the Magic Spell: Radical Theories of Folk and Fairy Tales*. Rev. and expanded ed. Lexington: University Press of Kentucky, 2002.

A groundbreaking collection of essays first published in 1979, this updated 2002 edition of Zipes's thought-provoking essays uses sociological and historical approaches to the analysis of fairy tales. He also explores morality and religion, not to mention Bettelheim and children's literature. Zipes's theories are bold and interesting, and even though this revised and expanded edition is now 10 years old, it challenges and intrigues me in fresh ways every time I read it. The chapter on Bettelheim's *The Uses of Enchantment* is unusually powerful and intellectually inspiring for readers looking to explore the controversial ideas of the infamous Dr. B.

———. *Why Fairy Tales Stick: The Evolution and Relevance of a Genre*. New York: Routledge, 2006.

One of my students' favorite research sources, *Why Fairy Tales Stick* digs into the reasons why people cannot seem to get enough of fairy tales and how intensely they have permeated popular world culture. Zipes investigates the literary aspects of fairy tales, their history, relevance, and importantly, for *Beyond the Glass Slipper*, why some tales are super popular and others are neglected. A scholarly work, first-year writing students find *Why Fairy Tales Stick* quite approachable, if challenging.

ABOUT THE EDITOR

Kate Wolford is editor and publisher of *Enchanted Conversation: A Fairy Tale Magazine* at fairytalemagazine.com. She teaches first-year college writing, incorporating fairy tales in her assignments whenever possible.

OTHER FAIRY TALE TITLES
FROM WORLD WEAVER PRESS

—

WOLVES AND WITCHES
A Fairy Tale Collection by
Amanda C. Davis and Megan Engelhardt

"Sisters Amanda C. Davis and Megan Engelhardt are the female Brothers Grimm." —K. Allen Wood, *Shock Totem*

Witches have stories too. So do mermaids, millers' daughters, princes (charming or otherwise), even big bad wolves. They may be a bit darker–fewer enchanted ball gowns, more iron shoes. Happily-ever-after? Depends on who you ask. In *Wolves and Witches*, sisters Amanda C. Davis and Megan Engelhardt weave sixteen stories and poems out of familiar fairy tales, letting them show their teeth.

"Dark and delicious revenge-filled tales! I Highly Recommend this fun and small collection of short stories."
—Fangs, Wands & Fairy Dust.

"A fabulous collection of re-imagined fairy tales. With their dark prose and evocative poetry these sisters have done the Brothers Grimm proud."
—Rhonda Parrish, *Niteblade Fantasy and Horror Magazine*

"A joy, start to finish."
—Mercedes M. Yardley, Author of *Beautiful Sorrows*

ALSO FROM WORLD WEAVER PRESS

Shards of History
Rebecca Roland

The Haunted Housewives of Allister, Alabama
A Cleo Tidwell Paranormal Mystery
Susan Abel Sullivan

Cursed: Wickedly Fun Stories
A Collection
Susan Abel Sullivan

Specter Spectacular: 13 Ghostly Tales
Anthology
Edited by Eileen Wiedbrauk

Forged by Fate
Fate of the Gods Trilogy: Book One
Amalia Dillin

———

Coming in 2013!

The King of Ash and Bone, and other stories
A Collection
Rebecca Roland

———

World Weaver Press
*Publishing fantasy, paranormal, and science fiction
that engages the mind and ensnares the story-loving soul.*

FATE OF THE GODS TRILOGY
From World Weaver Press

by Amalia Dillin

Every god, from each of the world's pantheons, mythologies, and religions — they're all real.

After Adam fell, God made Eve to protect the world.—Adam has pursued Eve since the dawn of creation, intent on using her power to create a new world and make himself its God. Throughout history, Eve has thwarted him, determined to protect the world and all of creation. Unknown to her, the Norse god Thor has been sent by the Council of Gods to keep her from Adam's influence, and more, to protect the interests of the gods themselves. But this time, Adam is after something more than just Eve's power — he desires her too, body and soul, even if it means the destruction of the world. Eve cannot allow it, but as one generation melds into the next, she begins to wonder if Adam might be a man she could love.

Forged by Fate
Fate of the Gods Trilogy: Book One

Tempting Fate—*coming in 2013!*
A Fate of the Gods Novella: (Book 1.5)

A Fate Forgotten—*coming in 2013!*
Fate of the Gods Trilogy: Book Two

Made in the USA
Middletown, DE
16 December 2014